The Government Shall Be Upon Whose Shoulder?

by
Mary M. O'Callaghan

The Government Shall Be Upon Whose Shoulder?
Copyright © 1999 by Mary M. O'Callaghan

ALL RIGHTS RESERVED

All Scripture references are from the Authorized King James Version of the Bible, unless otherwise marked.

References marked NKJ are from the New King James Version of the Bible, © copyright 1979, 1980, 1982 by Thomas Nelson, Inc., Nashville, Tennessee.

Published by:

Serenity Books

P.O. Box 3595
Hagerstown, MD 21742-3595

ISBN 1-884369-99-5

Printed in the United States of America
For Worldwide Distribution

Dedication

May this be a Praise Offering to the Glory of GOD, Creator of the Universe, to Whom the earth belongs, with all its fullness, and Whose I am.

May America continue to be a land of the free and a home of the brave, symbol of hope and freedom and justice and peace to a downtrodden and captive world.

Our fathers' God, to Thee,
Author of liberty,
To Thee we sing:
Long may our land be bright
With freedom's holy light;
Protect us by Thy might,
Great God, our King!

Acknowledgments

I pay tribute first of all to our American forefathers who, with purpose and vision, at the price of blood, sweat and tears, gave us a legacy of freedom to worship our God, if we will diligently preserve it against repressive government.

I thank Dr. Gwen R. Shaw, founder and President of End-Time Handmaidens and Servants, for her steadfast, godly example and training, truly a "Mother in Israel" (Judges 5:7).

I thank Pat Carver, President of Pat Carver International Ministries, for acclaiming this manuscript as "special — powerful, peace-giving, convicting, informing of the Gospel, loving, informing for families, challenging, and excellent!! It should be in every home in America!"

I honor Derek Prince for his dedicated, scholarly teaching that has influenced my life since I was first baptized in the Holy Spirit in 1972, at the age of fifty-two. So biblically based are his tapes and books that they are as applicable today as they were more than twenty-five years ago!

I acknowledge the debt of the entire Christian world to all those who established the International Christian Embassy in Jerusalem, regardless of earthly governments. As Ambassadors of Christ our home base is the City of the King of kings, to which Jesus will return to take His throne!

My special thanks go to the Rev. Fr. Paul Costopoulos, Greek Orthodox priest and very special friend of our daughter Wendy's family, now Dean of the Cathedral in Birmingham, who volunteered to sample this manuscript despite a very busy schedule. I appreciate his true Pastor's heart and his gracious encouragement to put this, my first literary collection, into print.

I thank God for my own Pastor, Rob Goyette, whose eyes reflect Jesus, whose ears hear His voice, whose feet follow the path of discipleship, whose hands minister the compassion of Christ to the congregation and the community, and whose heart pours forth the love of God. I appreciate the brief but precious monthly opportunities given me to share my love for Israel with the congregation.

I say thank you to the many friends through the years who have asked me to keep them on or add them to my Christmas list for these annual greetings. Friends are God's instruments for love.

And most of all, I thank God for His choice of a husband for me, and His bountiful blessings of six wonderful, loving children, children's children and children's children's children!

*The government shall be upon **HIS** shoulder.*
                              Isaiah 9:6

YE *are the* **BODY** *of* **CHRIST.**
                         I Corinthians 12:27

About the Author

Mary Mees launched her lifetime "Homemaker" career when her 1941 Phi Beta Kappa B.A. degree was superseded within twelve days by an "MRS." degree, conferring on her a new name, Mrs. L. J. (Jim) O'Callaghan. Over a sixteen-year period, five daughters and one son bestowed on her six "MA" degrees. Jim retired as Colonel, Air Force Reserves, on completing twenty years of military service. After World War II he founded a wholesale business in Atlanta. In time the family joined him in the political arena.

The six married children have extended the family to eighteen grandchildren and now six great-grandchildren! God was always central in the family. When Jim graduated to Glory in January 1997, Mary's "Homemaker" career took a literary bend to continue the fight to preserve godliness for all American families.

This, her first published work, chronicles life in America as we have allowed God to be gradually squeezed out of our government and culture. May it serve as a challenge to revive America so that all families can openly and publicly proclaim "IN GOD WE TRUST."

Contents

Preface 13
Foreword 15
Introduction 20
Commentary — 1958 22
Commentary — 1958-1963 25
Congressional Race — 1962 26
Update — 1998 29
Merry Christmas Newsletter — 1963 30
Fulton County Federation of Republican Women 33
National Elections, Campaign Issues — 1964 34
What's Happening to the Spirit of America? 44
Merry Christmas Newsletter — 1964 56
Commentary — 1998 on the '64 Elections 59
Post-election Letter to Forty-three
    Atlanta Area Clergymen and Educators 61
Commentary — 1998 and Two Letters from 1965 68
Christmas Newsletter — 1965 73
Commentary — 1965 75
Author's Note 78
Update — 1998 80
Christmas Greetings — 1966 81
Commentary — 1966 83
Commentary — 1967 84
Christmas Newsletter — 1967 86
Christmas Newsletter — 1968 89
Commentary — 1968 91
Update — 1998 91
Hallelujah! Christmas Newsletter — 1969 92
Commentary — 1969 94
Unpublished Letter to the Editor 95
Update — 1998 98

Christmas Newsletter — 1970	99
Commentary — 1970	101
Update — 1998	102
Interim Letter	103
Christmas Newsletter — 1971	106
Looking Back From 1998	108
Christmas Newsletter — 1972	109
O'Callaghan Christmas Greetings — 1973	112
It's Christmas Again — 1974!	114
Christmas 1975 — Naples, Florida	116
Commentary — The American Scene — to 1980	118
Christmas Greetings '76 — The Jim O'Callaghans	120
Fall Letter — 1977	122
Christmas Blessings — 1978; Aloft Over Wyoming	125
Christmas Greetings from the O'Callaghans in Naples — 1979	127
Commentary — 1998	129
Christmas Greetings from the O'Callaghans— 1980	131
Merry Christmas '81, from the Neapolitan O'Callaghan Clan	133
O'Callaghan Christmas Greetings, '82	135
A Couple's Marriage Is "A Series of Joys"	137
Merry Christmas from Naples — 1983!	139
America Through Christian Eyes — 1984	140
1984 Greetings from Mary and Jim O'Callaghan	143
Healing Scriptures in Behalf of Zachary Modlin	145
From Zachary's Parents	150
Happy Holy Days, The O'Callaghans — 1985	152
1986 Christmas Greetings — The O'Callaghans	154
O'Callaghan Merry Christmas — 1987	156
Joyous Christmas from Jacksonville — 1988	158
Holy Holidays — 1989	160
Celebrate the Christ in Christmas — 1990	162
Christmas Greetings from the Modlins	164
Christmas Joy — 1991, from Mary and Jim O'Callaghan	166
The Regas Family — 1991	168

Christmas 1992, The Regas Household 170
Be Blessed This Christmas, 1992!
  — Mary and Jim O'Callaghan 171
Modlins' Christmas Greetings — 1992 173
Mary's Family Letter 175
Merry Christmas '93, from the Modlins 177
O'Callaghan Greetings
  for Jesus' Birthday, 1993 179
A Soul's Prayer 181
Joy to You!! — 1994, Mary and Jim 182
Modlins' Christmas 1995 184
Merry Christmas — 1995; from Jim and Mary O'Callaghan ... 186
Christmas 1995 — from the Regases 188
Joyous Christmas — 1996,
  from Jim and Mary O'Callaghan 191
The Modlin Herald News — 1996 Edition 193
Merry Christmas 1996; from the Regas Family! 195
Unpublished Letter to *The Florida Times-Union* 198
"O Jerusalem, Jerusalem..." (Matthew 23:37)
  Mary O'Callaghan, November 1997 200
Merry Christmas; from Cindy and Bill MacNabb — 1998 202
Christmas Greetings; from the Underwoods! 204
Merry Christmas — 1998, from Mary O'Callaghan 206
December 1998 — The Regas family 208
Afterword 211
A Tribute 213
Year-End Commentary — 1998 218

Preface

Here we sit, somewhere in the midst of history! Certainly history does not start with us. But there *is* a beginning! Who can tell it? Who was there when history began? No mortal man!

Ah! There is an account of the beginning, before man was, handed down to us by God, the Author of history. He chose a special people for such a purpose! Today we call them the Jews. What a debt we owe them!

God, the Father of all, in His triune council with His Holy Spirit and His Word, brought forth the will of God — CREATION! Time began. History had begun! In the expanse of time, when one day was as a thousand years and a thousand years as one day, God commanded His universe into existence. Out of darkness He commanded light! Every successive expanse of day exploded with new creation. God's will was expressed by God's Word and empowered by God's Spirit — the totality of Divinity at work. God checked out each day's labor and pronounced it *good!*

On the sixth expansive day, Elohim God (*Elohim* is the plural form of the Hebrew word for God) said, *"Let Us make man in Our image, after Our likeness"* (Genesis 1:26). This was the epitome, different from all other creation! With His created man, God joined Heaven and Earth! He took the elements of the earth and formed them into the image of Himself. What a beautiful motionless and emotionless form! But God had a purpose for this form. It was to take dominion over His creation and subdue it. God breathed His breath into the nostrils of this form, face-to-face, and the form became Adam, man, a living soul, now in God's likeness! In man's completeness there was also triunity — a body that was made from the earth; a soul (i.e., a mind, a will and emotions to plan and execute God's will of dominion over the Earth); and a spirit, birthed from the very breath of God, through which he could communicate with his God! *Male and female created He them.* **Now** God called His creation *very good!*

The Hebrew word that expresses the oneness, the plural singularity, of Elohim God is *echad*, a word used daily by Jews the world over when they proclaim, *"Hear, O Israel: The* Lord *our God, the* Lord *is one! (echad)"* (Deuteronomy 6:4, NKJV). Those Jews who acknowledge Jesus as the prophesied and long-awaited Hebrew Messiah have no problem embracing the Son, along with the Father and the Holy Spirit, in the godly concept of *echad!* Genesis 2:24 reveals the meaning of *echad* in the natural context when husband and wife become *"one"* through the marriage covenant. Jesus told His disciples, *"I am in the Father, and the Father is in Me"* (John 14:11). Jesus assures them that when He goes back to the Father, He will send the Spirit of Truth to dwell with them and be in them. Because Jesus lives, we will live also, and in that day we will know that Jesus is in the Father, and He in us, and we in Him! (John 14:20.) What precious intimacy *echad* expresses, uniting God and His mankind!

Today we are living our brief lives in a minute portion of the time-space continuum. We can look back at the recorded beginnings and we can look ahead to God's end-time purposes through recorded prophecy when time will be no more! It was written *that we may know.* Our Father God does not want us to be ignorant! He has commissioned all of His people to tell everyone of His great plans and purposes, for His crowning desire has been for many sons and daughters to feast with Him at His banqueting table! FAMILY is God's ultimate purpose!

This book is based on a sliver of approximately forty years taken from current history in America as seen through the eyes of one family. May it delight and inspire you, as well as stir you to action to extend God's family throughout the Earth!

Mary M. O'Callaghan
Jacksonville, Florida

Foreword

History was never my favorite subject. Having passed the three score and ten mark, however, I find myself a part of history, which gives it new meaning and value! As a piece of antiquity, I can pontificate on the olden, golden days like an authority, because I lived them! How truly this was brought home to me when one of my granddaughters called long distance to interview me. It seems she was to question someone who had lived through the Great Depression and compare it with the current situation in America. I qualified!

No one will argue with the fact that life for mankind has changed more in the past seventy-five or eighty years than in all the previous years of history. Technology has not only given us ever more rapid modes of transportation and communication, extending us to the moon and beyond, but it has pierced the tiniest particles of matter to split the atom and to discover the DNA facts of life! Change in itself is not necessarily good or bad. It is what we do with it.

Two hundred and twenty-two years ago the United States of America was established as a "land of the free and home of the brave." It had been settled by those who risked all to escape religious persecution and governmental despotism. It became a symbol of "liberty and justice for all," to oppressed peoples the world over. God blessed this land as a land flowing with milk and honey, for *"blessed is the nation whose God is the LORD"* (Psalm 33:12). That means the God of Abraham, Isaac and Jacob, no other. These same past seventy-five or eighty years have also seen the greatest changes in American culture, I believe; some have been good and some have been very destructive.

In the midst of change, God changes not! I am grateful for the ROCK upon which our family is built, giving stability in the midst of the storms of life that are roaring around us. *"God setteth the solitary in families"* (Psalm 68:6). It is the family that is the building block of society. It is in the family that godly government is established, according to God's specific instructions and commandments.

Religion deals with people and rulership. Politics deals with people and rulership. There are some in America who have decried the mixing of politics and religion. The abuse of political power and the means of attaining it have given politics a dirty name. The time of statesmen sacrificing for the good of their country seems to have given way to career politicians who are entrenched at the public trough. The public media openly, ruthlessly and unashamedly make or break issues and candidates according to their own prejudices. The expenses of political campaigns have made it prohibitive for all but the wealthy to run for national office.

America has become a showcase of what happens when God-fearing people wash their hands of politics and of the political process. The small percentage of citizens who exercise the privilege of voting to choose their government is an indication of disinterest and disdain for politics and politicians. That is not to say that there aren't any godly, dedicated statesmen serving our nation in public office. But even godly candidates are asked, "What's in it for you? Why are you sticking your neck out to be lambasted and scrutinized by the public, while putting your family at the risk of unscrupulous political warfare?"

We are comfortable in the freedoms we have inherited from our self-sacrificing forefathers. We tend to forget the blood price that has been paid so that we might enjoy our God-given rights of choice. Freedom *is* choice. We have taken pride in the accomplishments of our nation under freedom, glad to reach out with helping hands to the oppressed of the world. But like the frog in the pot of water that is slowly coming to a boil, we have been slow to recognize the subtle changes in our society that are designed to cook us for someone's lunch! We relish the peace of our comfort zone and we discount as radically extreme the warnings of today's prophets. The comfortable cry, "We hate WAR! Let's eliminate the sounds of war from our hymnals! Let's be tolerant and embrace all religions, because God loves everybody!"

WHILE WE SIMMER, THE FIRE IS GETTING HOTTER! CAN YOU FEEL IT YET?

The second verse in the Bible, Genesis 1:2, informs us that Darkness was on the face of the deep and that God called forth Light, pronouncing it good. He divided the Light from the Darkness. From the beginning there has been a division between Darkness and Light. God called the light day and the darkness night. When the Word became flesh and dwelt among us, *"in Him was life and the life was the Light of men"* (John 1:4, NASB). That Light shines in the Darkness and the Darkness does not comprehend or apprehend it. When Jesus saw the man who had been blind from birth, He explained to His disciples that He must do the works of His Father while it was Day, for the Night was coming when no one could work. As long as He was in the world, He was *"the*

The Government Shall Be Upon Whose Shoulder?

Light of the world" (John 9:4,5, NKJV). Jesus urged them to believe "into" (the accurate Greek) the Light that they *"may become sons of Light"* (John 12:36, NASB).

You may note that I took the liberty of personifying Light and Darkness in some places. Jesus, our Savior, is Light, and Satan, our Adversary, deceptively transforms himself from Darkness into an angel, or messenger, of light (2 Corinthians 11:14). There has been an adversary, Satan, from the very beginning, which is why God told Adam to tend, or carefully guard, the garden. Jesus called this tempter the devil, a murderer from the beginning and the father of lies, as well as the prince of this world (John 8:44; 12:31). Those who today scoff at personified evil, or the devil, are branding God the liar! Such scoffers (including church denominations!) will be unable to cast out demons as Jesus did, because they have taken Satan's bait and have believed that demons and evil spirits belong to mythology or to the fantasies of primitive, unlearned cultures!

A most amazing fact of today's society is that many highly educated, well-positioned, sophisticated professionals and worldly brilliant leaders, and their followers, have embraced the deception of the New Age cult with its spirit guides, which are nothing more than the familiar spirits against which the Bible warns. This hidden and forbidden knowledge from the underworld lures the unsuspecting, as well as the rebellious, through television, telephone, literature, etc., with manifestations of demonic power and lying wonders. It perpetuates Satan's original sin and lie, puffing up with pride *"Hath God said?" "Ye shall not surely die." "Ye shall be as gods."* (Genesis 3:1, 4, 5.)

Either knowingly or unknowingly, New Agers are practicing witchcraft by channeling and searching for forbidden knowledge. The spirit realm is very real. Satan still lies! Psychic guides are his dark angels. Pretending to bring light, they bring death instead. Like Adam, New Agers have surrendered themselves to the authority of the devil. Perhaps the gory sacrifices, sadistic sexual rites, and every unthinkable filthy act of degradation practiced in witchcraft would horrify them, but New Agers have their feet caught in the same web! Only through the Holy Spirit by the power of the shed blood of Jesus and the authority of His Name can the Church extricate them from Satan's web! And an unbelieving church can never deliver victims from the demonic oppression that is the inevitable result of denying the truths of God's Word. An unbelieving church, in today's world of science, is somewhat to blame,

Mary M. O'Callaghan

having ignored or discounted the supernatural provisions in God's Word that make Him, and His will, clearly available to the believer.

An unbelieving church has tolerated the exile of God from America by government decree. Because of a misinterpretation by our Supreme Court of the intent of our Constitution, which was to allow for freedom for worship and prevent the establishment of a state church, God has been denied a place in America! Atheists have sued, and are continuing to sue thirty-five years later, under a pronouncement of separation of church from state, demanding equal rights with God! Their first victory was banning God from our public school systems. But the proof of the intentions of our Founding Fathers is clearly stated on all American monies, "IN GOD WE TRUST."

BOTH CHRISTIAN "FROGS" AND JEWISH "FROGS" HAVE STAYED IN THE POT TOGETHER, AGREEING WITH THE ATHEISTS THAT OUR LITTLE CHILDREN MUST BE PROTECTED FROM GOD.

The Bible itself and every symbol contained therein must be excluded from public view, because the God of Abraham, Isaac and Jacob is intolerant of other gods, thereby usurping the rights of all unbelievers! It is amazing that the principle of protecting the rights of the individual from the majority seems to extend to everyone but a godly believer! The courts refuse to allow even silent meditation or bowing of the head, lest it offend someone! Is no one afraid of offending God? Sadly, the fear of man outweighs the fear of God in humanistic America.

Though our system of justice has been based on godly principles, and oaths of office are administered with the oath taker's right hand upon the Bible while affirming, "So help me God," our courts have even ruled that it is illegal to display the Ten Commandments in our schools. With years of liberal Congresses, no one has demanded the impeachment of the Supreme Court justices for their ungodly and unconstitutional decisions, though it was the right and duty of Congress to do so.

Would it surprise you to know that America has established a "state religion" despite the First Amendment to our Constitution which prohibits such? Our Supreme Court has officially designated "secular humanism" as a religion! For years secular humanism has been and continues to be taught and practiced throughout our public school systems! Halloween, the high holy day of Satanists and witches, can be celebrated with impunity in our schools; yet every Judeo-Christian symbol and celebration has been banned from all public institutions.

The Government Shall Be Upon Whose Shoulder?

HAVE WE NOT EYES TO SEE, OR ARE WE GETTING SO PARBOILED WE CAN THINK ONLY OF OURSELVES AND OURS?

The Church of Jesus Christ has been called to be light and salt in the earth. Instead, apathy, ignorance, unbelief and lack of love for the lost, for differing denominations and for the Jewish roots of our faith have contributed to the present condition of our nation. The Lamb of God who freely poured forth His blood to take away the sins of the world has been publicly vilified as something common and vulgar. Unprincipled rulers have tolerated the use of our tax money for the purpose of insulting the very Giver of Life. These same lawmakers refuse to tolerate the freedom of speech, which includes the rights of school graduates to mention God and to pray in the valedictory addresses. Why do I blame the Church, of which I am a part? Because the world certainly can't be expected to uphold the honor of God if the Church is delinquent in doing so!

THE HEAT HAS BEEN TURNED UP AND THE WATER IS GETTING HOTTER UNDER US. WE HAVE BEGUN TO RECOGNIZE THE DANGER AND ARE STRENGTHENING OUR LIMBS TO JUMP OUT OF THE POT BEFORE IT IS TOO LATE! I AM AFRAID A PART OF THE CHURCH WILL BE LEFT BEHIND IN THE POT, PREFERRING THE HEAT TO THE FELLOWSHIP OF POT-JUMPERS!

Introduction

Welcome to an interpretive exposé on the critical years in America from the early nineteen sixties as lived out by one active Southern American family. Rejoice with their annual Christmas celebrations and weep with their sorrows as presented by this American mother — turned grandmother and now great-grandmother — and family members! Interspersed with letters are commentaries on the political situation and how the American family has been affected by it.

May I introduce to you the Jim O'Callaghan family. Jim, or L.J., was a native Atlantan who put himself through Georgia Tech with a newspaper route. When he graduated in 1937 he got one of the better jobs, which was paying $300 a month. That same year Mary graduated from high school in Atlanta, having moved there with her family from Charlotte, North Carolina. Four years later, and twelve days after graduating from Randolph-Macon Woman's College in Lynchburg, Virginia, Mary's Methodist pastor and Jim's Presbyterian pastor joined them together in Holy Matrimony. It was June 14, 1941. Jim was serving his required one year of active duty as a Reserve officer at the Orlando Air Base. But Pearl Harbor occurred in December of 1941, and Jim's year of active duty stretched into five by the end of World War II. While Jim helped "win the war" in the Pacific, Mary stayed in Atlanta with their firstborn "Marky" (Mary Kathryn) and son "Jimbo." After the war, Jim started Dealers Supply Company, Incorporated, a wholesale heating and air-conditioning business, along with a related manufacturing company. He continued his Reserve military duties, retiring as a Colonel after twenty years of service.

Karen was the third to put in her appearance, three and a half years after Jimbo, and two years later Cindy made four! As Cindy approached school age, Marky suggested it was time for another baby in the family. Parents concurred, and Wendy arrived to be Marky's special little project. When Laurie graced the scene two years later, Marky protested, "I didn't ask for but one!" Wendy took a look at her replacement, who was in Mama's lap, and commanded, "Send her back!" Jimbo's response after the fifth sister was, "Crummy family." He eventually learned to appreciate being the only boy, having a room of his own! They still accuse Laurie of being spoiled, but isn't that universal for the last chick in the nest? Dad managed to gracefully give away his daughters in marriage,

The Government Shall Be Upon Whose Shoulder?

until the very last one flew the coop, leaving the nest empty. Who said grown men don't cry?

Besides three successive toy poodles, Chopper, Rafferty and Skipper, you will be introduced to Mary's mother, called BooBoo (for Beulah), and her aunt Marnie, and Jim's mother, called May-Ma by the grandchildren, and his Aunt Ceal from Nashville, Tennessee. Mary's older siblings are Curtis and Don Mees, and Dot Kendrick. Jim's are older brother Bill, and younger Richard, Katharine Lorenz and Ben.

The spouses, along with eighteen grandchildren and a growing number of great-grandchildren, will be introduced as they arrive on the scene.

Commentary — 1958

Fasten your seat belt and prepare for takeoff, back to December of 1958! While on a business trip with his partner, Jim underwent emergency surgery at the Jewish Hospital in Cincinnati for a ruptured appendix, with ensuing peritonitis and gangrene. Mary left the two youngest girls with Jim's married sister, and Marky (who was age fifteen) took charge of the others in Atlanta, under the watchful eyes of their grandmothers.

It was two degrees above zero when Mary climbed off the overnight train in Cincinnati. Feeling the need to stretch her legs, this Southern girl started to walk the several blocks from the hotel to the hospital, carrying Jim's little suitcase with his extra pajamas, etc. Her hand didn't actually freeze to the handle of that little suitcase, but it might have if a little store that was about halfway there hadn't been open!

This first letter is addressed to the six children, ages one to fifteen, during Jim's three and a half weeks of hospitalization.

Politically, at this time Jim was finishing his first year of a four-year term on the Atlanta Board of Education. A year or two earlier he had made an unsuccessful bid for the Georgia State Legislature. He was an unknown and ran third in a three-man race. Even his friends asked him why he, a businessman and a graduate of Georgia Tech, wanted to get involved in politics. Since his business was well enough established for him to take some time off, Jim followed his firm conviction that government should not be left to professional politicians and lawyers only, but that Christian businessmen should exercise their responsibility in government, even if it meant sacrifice. He never believed in asking someone else to do what he himself would not do. That involvement is even more critical today!

Georgia was a one-party, Democratic state run by a county unit system, which virtually disenfranchised the big-city Atlanta voters. Citizens were not registered by party, but were simply registered as voters. Most of the political rallies in Atlanta in those days were held in the Negro churches. The press would be there, and it was important to have your name and platform positions presented to the voters. An offering would always be received, and candidates were reminded of certain needs in the church! We were learning the facts of Georgia politics! One fact was

The Government Shall Be Upon Whose Shoulder?

that the friends Jim thought he could count on for support in that first race had previously committed themselves to another candidate by the time he had entered the race. The press didn't quote the other losing candidate when he appealed to the voters who were present in the church, "My skin may be white, but I want you to know my heart is just as black as yours!"

It was shortly after this initial, unsuccessful venture that some friends urged Jim to run with a slate of candidates for the Atlanta Board of Education, to break up what was probably the most powerful political entity in the state. This they did, and from the day they were sworn in office they were under court order to plan, and implement, the desegregation of the Atlanta school system. Desegregation was eventually carried out without incident in Atlanta, despite the Governor's determination to close schools rather than comply. The first year, they desegregated the top high school grades, prohibiting any outside personnel from stepping onto school grounds. Lower grades were added each year until all were covered. Unfortunately, education became secondary to socialization and "values clarification." The values that were "clarified" were those of our biblically founded moral code, which was now denied acceptance in our schools.

The letter:

Jewish Hospital
Cincinnati, Ohio
December 22, 1958

My Darling Children,

I hope there will not be many Christmases when we'll be separated, because Christmas is a precious time for families to celebrate together our Saviour's birth. But I am thankful for the opportunity to send you a Christmas message and remind you of the real significance and deep meaning of Christmas. It is the most important event of history, and a most incredible event when you consider that God Himself, loving mankind as He did, came upon this Earth for a brief spell to teach us once and for all what He wanted from us and to promise us in no uncertain way an eternity with Him after our brief life here.

As science probes into space and God reveals more of His wonders to us,

Mary M. O'Callaghan

can we doubt what Jesus said when He said, "In My Father's house are many mansions, and I go to prepare a place for those who love Me and follow Me"? Could anything be more earthshaking than God with us, right here on Earth, Emmanuel? Jesus came to show us how to love, not just those people we like and look up to, but all mankind, all races, our enemies, the weak and unattractive, the spoiled and selfish, the sinners. When we have compassion and love in our hearts, then and only then, will we know the peace that God promises to men of good will. Then we really understand that God is love.

This gift of God is the most precious gift you will ever have. Cherish it, nourish it, study it, so that it will increase in meaning; even doubt it, because it will withstand any doubting, questioning or testing you may put it to. Because God gave us such a gift, it has become our custom to celebrate by giving gifts to those we love, by remembering our friends, and by sharing our blessings. But we can't outgive God, so don't ever let our gift giving overshadow the real meaning of Christmas.

Dedicate yourself to serving God and mankind in whatever may be your walk in life — housewife, doctor, scientist, businessman — and your life will be rich and rewarding. Men change, situations change, but God will never change from what He has revealed to us in Jesus Christ. It will be hard for you little ones to understand this; sometimes we grown-ups even forget. But keep it in your hearts and someday you'll know what I mean!

So you see, Daddy and I don't really need a Christmas tree and presents and bright lights to feel the spirit of Christmas. We carry it in our hearts, first the love of God, then of each other and our wonderful family.

You all have been wonderful to carry on and do all the hectic preparations without us. We are sorry to have to miss one precious moment of it. We can be so thankful your Daddy is doing and feeling better. Give May-Ma, BooBoo and Marnie some extra special love from us, because I am sure they are sad to miss the loved ones they have enjoyed Christmases with. Love and take care of each other always, as you are doing now. And a very Merry Christmas to each one of you!

In His love,
Mother and Daddy

Commentary — 1958-1963

From Christmas 1958 we span the years to Christmas 1963, with greetings sent to kissin' kin and kissin' friends. Jim continued the remaining three years of his term on the Atlanta Board of Education, serving as President for one year, despite a serious heart attack in March 1960. This was the year he would turn forty-five, so he had happily started competing in Seniors Tennis, but the tennis racquet had to be swapped for the slower-paced golf clubs. Following his heart attack, Jim determined that his wholesale heating and air-conditioning business must be able to continue independently of him, or he would have nothing to leave for his family. Consequently, he turned the reins over to his brother Richard, and Jim became Chairman of the Board. Jim never went back to full-time service. Instead, he started an entirely new career with Courts and Company, a New York Stock Exchange firm.

Politically, Georgia was a one-party state, run by county politics, with the typical results that come from a lack of competition. For years, political success required allegiance to that party. Besides, Grandpa might turn over in his grave if one voted otherwise! The Democratic party had long since set up rules which hindered, if not prevented, competition of any kind, so that the primary was tantamount to election. Their rules required that a certain number of signatures on petitions were necessary to place a name on the ballot in any particular race in which a party had not presented a candidate for the previous election. Some undaunted Republicans promised much aid and assistance if Jim would agree to run for Congress in 1962. The signatures were gathered, fees paid, issues studied, and we were off and running in behalf of a two-party system. We didn't win the election, but we won in that we didn't have to move our family to Washington to live!

Congressional Race — 1962

Over many years now, the Congressional Record and the published works of ex-Communists have revealed the Communist timetables for world dominion, including specific goals aimed at America. Satan's battlefield is the mind of man, so psychological warfare is his method and words are his tools. Just as the Word of God is the sword of the Spirit, so the word of deception is Satan's aggressive weapon. His slogans are disarmingly idealistic and the constant doses subtly render their poisons, so that mental attitudes change gradually and imperceptibly to reach out and embrace revolution and destruction.

As a candidate for congressional office, it was necessary and urgent to study the *stated* goals of the enemy of America. Not to do so was, and is, to stick one's head in the sand. As a guardian of the faith, it behooves every Believer to determine for himself the progress of these stated Communist goals. It behooves every American who desires to protect his freedoms, be he a Believer or not, to study these goals and determine the price he is willing to pay to preserve his heritage.

1. U.S. acceptance of coexistence as the only alternative to atomic war.
2. U.S. willingness to capitulate, in preference to engaging in atomic war.
3. Develop the illusion that total disarmament by the U.S. would be a demonstration of moral strength.
4. Permit free trade between all nations regardless of Communist affiliation and whether or not items could be used for war.
5. Extension of long-term loans to Russia and her satellites.
6. Provide American aid to all nations regardless of Communist domination.
7. Grant recognition of Red China and admission to the U.N.
8. Set up East and West Germany as separate states, regardless of promised free elections supervised by the U.N.
9. Prolong conferences to ban atomic tests, since America suspends testing while conferring.
10. Give all Soviet satellites individual representation in the U.N., despite size and population.

The Government Shall Be Upon Whose Shoulder?

11. Promote the U.N. as the only hope of mankind.
12. Resist all attempts to outlaw the Communist party.
13. Eliminate all loyalty oaths.
14. Continue to give Russia access to the U.S. Patent Office.
15. Capture one, or both, of the political parties in the U.S.
16. Use technical decisions of the courts to weaken basic American institutions by claiming their activities violate civil rights.
17. Get control of the schools. Use them as transmission belts for socialism and current Communist propaganda. Soften the curriculum. Get control of the teachers' associations. Put the party line in textbooks.
18. Gain control of all student newspapers.
19. Use student riots to foment public protests against programs or organizations that are under Communist attack.
20. Infiltrate the press. Get control of book-review assignments, editorial writing, and policy-making positions.
21. Gain control of key positions in radio, TV and motion pictures.
22. Continue discrediting American culture by degrading all forms of artistic expression. An American Communist cell was told to "eliminate all good sculpture from parks and buildings; substitute shapeless, awkward and meaningless forms."
23. Promote ugliness and repulsive, meaningless art by controlling art critics and directors of art museums.
24. Eliminate all laws governing obscenity by calling them censorship and a violation of free speech and free press.
25. Break down cultural standards of morality by promoting pornography and obscenity in books, magazines, motion pictures, radio and TV.
26. Present homosexuality, degeneracy and promiscuity as "normal, natural, healthy."
27. Infiltrate the churches and replace revealed religion with "social" religion. Discredit the Bible and emphasize the need for intellectual maturity, which does not need a "religious crutch."
28. Eliminate prayer, or any phase of religious expression, in the schools on the ground that it violates the principle of "the separation of church and state."

29. Discredit the American Constitution by calling it inadequate, old-fashioned, out-of-step with modern needs, a hindrance to cooperation between nations on a worldwide basis.
30. Discredit the American Founding Fathers. Present them as selfish aristocrats who had no concern for the "common man."
31. Belittle all forms of American culture and discourage the teaching of American history on the ground that it was only a minor part of the big picture.
32. Support any socialist movement that will give centralized control over any part of U.S. culture, education, social agencies, welfare programs, mental health clinics, etc.
33. Eliminate all laws or procedures that interfere with the operation of the Communist apparatus.
34. Eliminate the House Committee on Un-American Activities.
35. Discredit and eventually dismantle the FBI.
36. Infiltrate and take control of more unions.
37. Infiltrate and take control of big business.
38. Transfer some of the powers of arrest from the police to the social agencies. Treat all behavioral problems as psychiatric disorders which no one but a psychiatrist can understand or treat.
39. Dominate the psychiatric profession and use mental health laws as a means of gaining coercive control over those who oppose Communist goals.
40. Discredit the family as an institution. Encourage promiscuity and easy divorce.
41. Emphasize the need to raise children away from the negative influence of parents. Attribute prejudices, mental blocks and retarding of children to the suppressive influence of parents.
42. Create the impression that violence and insurrection are legitimate aspects of the American tradition; that students and special-interest groups should rise up and use "united force" to solve economic, political, or social problems.
43. Overthrow all colonial governments before native populations are ready for self-government.
44. Internationalize the Panama Canal.
45. Give the World Court jurisdiction over nations and individuals.

Update — 1998

The above listed Communist goals were available for study before the 1962 elections. Senator William Knowland placed this plan captured from an American Communist cell in the Congressional Record. It may be found under April 29, 1964, on page 5708.

These commentaries, which are designed to bridge the gap between the letters, were originally written in 1984. As I updated them for the current publication, I was astounded by the progress that has been made in the past fourteen years in accomplishing these goals to destroy American sovereignty! The Iron Curtain may have fallen, but it seems to have fallen right in the midst of the United States! Why is Gorbachev headquartered in the Presidio in San Francisco at taxpayers' expense? Why is the current Administration giving American land and river rights to the U.N. without the approval of Congress or the people? Why is the control of the Panama Canal being relinquished while Communist China is establishing itself at both ends of the canal? Behind-the-scenes negotiations to lease to China our naval base on the West Coast were countered in time for Congress to block them. Unpublicized presidential Executive Orders, intended to protect America in times of crisis, are being used to overrule the sovereign will of the people. The Trojan horse has been welcomed to our land! They said we would even vote it in! The National Council of Churches echoes the agenda, undermining biblical values. The Bible warns of little foxes spoiling the vine, but America is encountering wolves, bears and dragons! When is the Church going to wake up and protect the family, God's building block, and demand, "Enough is enough!"?

Merry Christmas Newsletter — 1963

Jingle bells and holly wreaths,
    And friends both far and near
Remind us of the blessings
    Of this season, held so dear,
When God in Person came on Earth
    And dwelt among us here.

And now we join the happy voices
    Singing joy and mirth
In celebration everywhere
    Of our dear Saviour's birth,
Which gives to you and me and all
    An undeserved worth.

A love like God's we really
    Cannot fully understand.
This world's events would make us think
    That man does not love man.
But Christ on Earth has shown us
    Just what love must do, and can!

We have a job, as sons of God;
    We have a job to do,
To love the world, the good, the bad,
    And the indifferent, too.
Till all the world loves all the rest,
    We know we'll not be through.

The O'Callaghans have had a fine year in 1963 — no politics, no heart attacks, no babies, no weddings, a few nice trips, and everyone is in school!
    Jimbo decided he wanted to get back to the big city, and transferred himself to Emory University after a semester at Davidson, a Presbyterian College near

The Government Shall Be Upon Whose Shoulder?

Charlotte, North Carolina, my old hometown where I lived until we moved to Atlanta when I was fourteen. He's very happy and has pledged Kappa Alpha, which pleased Marky, since she thinks they are "the greatest."

Marky will graduate from Emory in March and is now looking for an exciting and munificent job. As President of her Tri-Delta chapter she enjoyed a convention trip to Colorado, with a few days in the Windy City. She volunteered one session of counseling at Camp Calvin, our Presbyterian camp where Jimbo served on staff all summer.

Karen went to summer school with a friend in Decatur. (Maybe the boys were cuter there!) Though only a junior, she works on the staff of the Northside High School Annual and holds office in several school clubs. She strums the guitar, as do most sixteen-year-olds, and has been singing with a couple boys at a pizza place on high school football nights. They call themselves "The Villagers," and are really quite good. She serves as President of our Senior High Dept. at Central Presbyterian Church, and they and the Pioneers will thaw out here Sunday night with hot chocolate and doughnuts after caroling for shut-ins.

Cindy still plays the flute in the school band and is now a bona fide freshman (ninth grade). She's the organized one in the family, making sure we get where we are supposed to, when we are supposed to, without forgetting anyone. (Twice have we left someone at church as the other seven of us piled into the car without a nose count.) She always manages to have plenty of baby-sitting money.

Wendy turned eight this month with a roller skating party. She loves being a Brownie. Laurie, at six, is thrilled with learning to read for herself. Since she is in school until 1:45, I have resumed my art correspondence course, though slowly. Working on two church councils and teaching in the Senior High Department leave little spare time for me. But who's complaining?

Jim is thoroughly enjoying managing the Mutual Funds Department at Courts and Company. He was in Boston with about thirty men that he had taken there for training when they received word that President Kennedy had been shot. Of course, everything closed down immediately. He has just now returned from New York, where he took about twenty more. We enjoyed a Mutual Funds conference this fall at Miami Beach, as well as our biennial jaunt to New Orleans when Georgia Tech plays Tulane. Those chocolate éclairs, beignets and delicacies from Antoine's, Brennan's, Commanders Palace, etc., make it imperative to avoid using the scales for a few weeks!

Mary M. O'Callaghan

This spring I took Jim's mother, Aunt "Ceal" from Nashville, and our two youngest to Redington Beach, Florida, near St. Petersburg for our annual visit. Jim brought Karen, Cindy and two of their cousins down when school was out, so I had a whole month of sunning and shelling. There is nothing like the Gulf Coast of Florida! Jim's sister, Katharine Lorenz, joined us from her home in Vero Beach. MayMa lives for this trip every year, and I am the official chauffeur. She broadcasts the glories of her Shangri-La to all who will listen, but she won't tell when we are going, so that we'll have no interlopers! I must admit, when she is ready, I am ready to take off too!

Jim continues to golf several times a week, but it takes too much time for me. We do have a new addition to the family, "Chopper," a scraggly black and white toy poodle, about one pound soaking wet. He's the dearest and sweetest little pet we have ever had.

But that's enough about us. Now we'd like to hear all about you and your family.

Happy New Year!
Mary and Jim,
Marky, Jimbo, Karen, Cindy, Wendy, Laurie, and "Chopper"

Fulton County Federation of Republican Women

(God Bless the Anonymous Author)

AND THE GREATEST OF THESE IS LOVE
(PARAPHRASE OF 1 CORINTHIANS 13)

Though I speak with ease and brilliance before large groups of women, and have not love for the individual woman in my heart, my words are empty and I am nothing.

And though I have a thorough knowledge of women's work and understand my organization fully, and have not love for the people it is meant to serve, I gain nothing.

And though I attend countless meetings and give unlimited hours of my time, and have not a personal and loving relationship with God, I am nothing.

Love is patient with the weakness of others; it is not irritable or rude. Love does not insist on its own way; it is able to take criticism without being unduly hurt.

Love does not need recognition or acclaim for its labors. Love is not aware of social position or lack of it; it does not hear gossip.

Love reaches out to touch the best qualities in each woman. Love never gives up seeking answers to the thorniest problems, and love gives the strength and endurance to work out their solutions.

Love and the work that love does will never end. When I was a child I spoke like a child, I read childish literature and in general lived life on a lighter level. But now I am a mature woman and I am responsible to think deeply about life and to invest my hours and days wisely and well.

For now as we see things in the uncertain light of this world, we are often confused and frustrated and discouraged; but then, in the pure light of eternity, we shall see the threads of our work woven into a pattern of everlasting beauty and value.

And now we have faith in God, hope for the future of the humanity we serve, and love for God and one another; and the greatest of these is Love.

National Elections, Campaign Issues — 1964

After recuperating from the excoriation that only a Republican would receive from the Atlanta newspapers, Jim and Mary attended the Republican National Convention in San Francisco as observers, when Barry Goldwater became the Republican Presidential nominee. Proof of the way words can create or destroy was the gross distortion by the liberal press of Goldwater's use of the word "extremism," even in the defense of liberty.

Today, the same press does not choose to attack sodomy, abortion, adultery, homosexuality, Satan worship, etc., as "extreme." Rather, they affirm these aberrations, as well as the Administration that classifies them as legally protected, "politically correct," even seeking special privileges for such practitioners as "legal minorities"! The media continue to try to brainwash the public into accepting the idiocy that burning and desecrating the American flag is merely a form of "free speech." At any criticism of their distorted views they scream "censorship," while they attack every expression of Judeo-Christian morality in the public arena as illegal. They censor our right of free speech with impunity! A teacher with a closed Bible on his desk is liable to censure, to firing and to legal suit in a system of politically activist judges and courts.

Thankful that they had completed their stint in the political process, Jim and Mary returned to Atlanta, only to discover that an untried newcomer had paid his qualifying fee to enter the Fifth District Congressional race. Too much was at stake to leave it to the unknown, so Jim again took up the challenge, producing the first Republican primary in modern years in this Democratic state. At least a viable two-party system was produced in Georgia, which was the main goal! With success in the primary came more months of study and hard work.

Republican Headquarters sent informational bulletins to Congressional candidates highlighting specific needs for legislation. One such three-page bulletin from 1964 has miraculously been preserved and just now surfaced, after family moves from Atlanta to Naples, Florida, and to Jacksonville; after reducing the family of eight down to two, and then to one, after Jim's death in January 1997. The headline reads:

The Government Shall Be Upon Whose Shoulder?
Ways Our Freedoms Can Be Lost

Emphasize that the loss of freedom to big government is **slow** and **subtle**, that freedoms are not lost overnight. These losses involve:

- Freedom of action
- Freedom of information
- Invasion of privacy

The Farmer

Spy in the sky:

Various methods of production already limit the freedom of action of farmers. In the agricultural sector, Orville Freeman (U.S. Secretary of Agriculture) has invaded the privacy of farmers by sending photographic spy planes over eighty percent of the nation's farmlands to determine if acreage allotments are being exceeded. Such federal snooping violates the privacy of the individual.

Jail sentences for farmers:

In the original draft of the 1963 farm legislation, Orville Freeman actually demanded jail sentences for farmers who did not keep records the way he wanted them to be kept. This has not become a loss of freedom, because the provision was defeated before farm legislation was enacted into law. But it could well be a part of subsequent legislation.

Agriculture Department wire:

Farmers are subject to the propaganda activities of Orville Freeman by the use of federal tax dollars and the implementation of the Department of Agriculture's wire service, which is designed to slant farm news and farm prices.

Wheat dumping:

Wheat dumping has violated the farmers' right to operate in the open market place. Over 70 million bushels of wheat have been dumped on the domestic market since July 1, at the minimum legal price, $1.37. Last year this figure was $1.76.

Wheat farmers throughout the nation rejected the big government legislation solutions. Despite their overwhelming opposition, virtually the same bill was enacted and now regulates wheat production. Orville Freeman promised "more freedom for farmers," but this legislation proves conclusively his goal of limiting freedom for farmers.

Business

Filling out forms:

The Federal Government has over five thousand forms in use for regular reporting — not including reports to the IRS and other agencies of the Treasury Department. The individual forced to cope with these forms is robbed of his time and is forced to make unwanted expenditures of money and personnel to comply with the big government's appetite for information.

NLRB:

The National Labor Relations Board ruled that a South Carolina firm, which could no longer operate competitively, could not go out of business. The NLRB ordered the former stockholders and the stockholders of companies that had had an interest in the defunct business to pay seven million dollars in back wages to employees. The power to determine private economic decisions — such as going out of business — is NOT within the purview of the Federal Government.

The NLRB ruled that a Chicago firm may not administer an aptitude test to prospective employees, because an aptitude test tends to discriminate against Negroes, who are "constantly discriminated against" and do therefore have an inferior background. This is clearly a violation of the employer's right to select the best man for the job.

Steel price:

When steel prices were raised, this Administration practiced direct intimidation by threatening tax suits against steel companies and executives. The government's "wage-price guidelines" emerged from the steel incident, and these guidelines interfere with the free market mechanism.

Forced integration:

Defense Secretary McNamara has attempted to force integration in business establishments located near military bases. He has done this by ordering Base Commanders to place "off-limits" all establishments practicing segregation.

FEPC:

The Federal Government seeks a national law to police businesses with twenty-five employees or more, in order to regulate mixing practices; partially achieved by the Civil Rights Act, whose hiring practices (or FEPC) section will apply to such in 1969.

Justice Department

Newsmen, commentators, businessmen, and others who have questioned the investigative and coercive tactics of Robert Kennedy's Justice Department have been threatened with tax investigations and prosecutions if they do not accede to the Justice Department's demands. This violates the basic right of Americans to question and to dissent.

News Media

Right to lie:

The government has infringed upon the right to information and the right to know by stating flatly, in the words of Arthur Sylvester, that government has a **"right to lie"** to save itself.

Billie Sol Estes and Bobby Barker cases:

Freedom of information and the right to know are again violated by a cover-up of the Billie Sol Estes and Bobby Baker cases. The Executive Branch has used every means at its disposal to sweep these cases under the rug and to deny the American people their basic right to information.

Mary M. O'Callaghan

Government Competition

The Federal Government competes directly with private business by running thousands of commercial-industrial enterprises. It has, for example, one-hundred agencies in the business of insuring, lending and guaranteeing credit for farming, housing, foreign trade, foreign investment and even domestic commerce and industry.

Communities and States

The Federal Government has the power to grant or deny millions of dollars to communities and states, depending on whether or not government rules are accepted (school funds, ARA [Area Redevelopment Administration] housing). At the whim of a federal bureaucrat, tax dollars, which belong to a state, may be denied it.

Supreme Court

Through invasion and usurpation of the prerogatives of the other COEQUAL branches of government, the Supreme Court, in fact, denies equal protection by the law — thus violating the Constitution.

(End of bulletin)

Few American citizens today remember what life was like in the pre-Franklin D. Roosevelt days, when the poison of socialism began to be injected into American life. Slowly but steadily it has done its work to destroy our freedoms and the basic tenets of our moral fiber. The God of Abraham, Isaac and Jacob, in Whom we claim to trust, has been denied His place in American history and life. When the standard has been destroyed, there is no justice, and everyone does what is right in his own eyes. Good is being called evil, and evil is being called good. America is ripe for the wrath of God's judgment, which has been pronounced upon sin. God will not be mocked.

Bible reading and prayer in schools were declared unconstitutional by the Supreme Court in 1963, so it was still very much an issue in the 1964 campaigns. Congress is supposed to wield the legislative power, not the Supreme Court (though that seems to have been forgotten, even today). The foremost issue in Mary's heart was the denial of God in any part of American life.

The Government Shall Be Upon Whose Shoulder?

The Becker Amendment, authored by both parties, sought to restore the **right** of the **people** to **choose** whether or not they wanted prayer and Bible reading in their districts. Congressman Becker thought it was such an important issue, that our children not grow up in a godless society like the communists', he gave up his office to work full time and to see to it that America retained that right of choice, despite the Supreme Court's ungodly interpretations and pronouncements.

Mary was invited to speak at a ladies' meeting on behalf of Jim's congressional candidacy, along with Mrs. Weltner, the wife of the Democratic incumbent (whom he later divorced to marry one of his campaigners). What a surprise it was to find that it was not Mrs. Weltner, but a very popular journalist from the Atlanta newspapers, Doris Lockerman, who presented the Democratic side. Mary's letter to Doris follows:

October 3, 1964

Dear Doris,

It was a pleasure to be with you the other evening and I sincerely thank you for your gracious and warm remarks about Jim. They say a thin-skinned person should not be in politics, but a person who is sensitive enough to the needs of others to offer himself for public service cannot help but be sensitive when his own person is maligned for political gain. Your kind and sincere words did provide some balm for past and for undoubtedly forthcoming "cuts." Since you and your family have experienced persecutions from irresponsible people, you can imagine how doubly shocking it is to be the victim of attack from supposedly responsible elements of society. I cannot help but judge your editor as a deterrent to good government because his practiced political actions do keep good and conscientious men from offering. I am honestly flattered that he would think I am such a threat to his candidate that he would send his star writer to debate me! Thank you again for graciously setting me at ease and being so generous in your remarks.

There were two things you said that concerned and disturbed me deeply and I can't help but urge you to consider them further, because I know you are motivated by the same Christian principles as I. One is "that our goal in life is and must be peace." If this is so, you nullify the very purpose for dying of every single man

Mary M. O'Callaghan

and woman who has ever given his life for the cause of liberty. At the opening of a Geneva Conference with Western powers in 1954 Secretary of State Dulles said, "Peace is always easy to achieve — by surrender. Unity is also easy to achieve — by surrender. The hard task that confronts us is to combine peace and unity with freedom."

Christ said, "Peace is My parting gift to you, My own peace such as the world cannot give. Let not your heart be troubled nor let it fear." That was before He sent His followers into the world to tell the Good News and thereby face persecution — certainly not peace as the world knows it. Death faces us all and we must not panic at the prospect of someone "pushing the button." What we must be concerned with is the insidious plot to capture the world for the forces of evil that attempt to blot out the Good News. Thank God for the sure knowledge that He is in control of His universe and will always preserve a remnant to proclaim the Gospel, no matter what judgment may be brought upon godless nations! Our faithfulness to His cause MUST be the only driving force of our lives and the task is being ignored by His followers who seek personal security. There is no security without God.

Since you are a former member of the FBI, I'm sure you have read J. Edgar Hoover's book, *Masters of Deceit*, published in 1958. I have not studied it thoroughly, but here are a few excerpts regarding the real nature of communism: "For the member, religion is not a private affair. No tolerance is allowed... The Party is working desperately to mold atheistic materialism as a weapon of revolution which, if it is to succeed, must first sap religion's spiritual strength and then destroy it." And in four steps he tells the Party's attack to assure total victory of atheistic communism over religion. He explains that the first or lower stage of communism (socialism) is the "impure" communist society, fresh from the violent conflict. Police, army, etc., are necessary under the dictatorship of the proletariat, crushing the opposition of the bourgeoisie. The higher or final stage (communism) will be reached when all capitalistic characteristics have been purged. This stage will be stateless, classless and godless, where property is held in common and the principle is "from each according to his abilities, to each according to his needs."

Mrs. Lockerman, this last principle sounds so dangerously like the "leveling off" of society, which you advocated with the Democrats. It frightens me that you could have been reached by such a philosophy, for I know you to be an intelligent

The Government Shall Be Upon Whose Shoulder?

Christian woman. Individuals must be inspired to cultivate their talents and reach for the stars, with the sure knowledge that each human being is different, with different capabilities and talents and motivations. It is this guarantee, to be different, that we must preserve. God does not judge us by the number of talents we possess, for these were gifts bestowed by Him, but by the faithfulness with which we use them to glorify Him. He even assures us that to those who have will more be given, whereas from the faithless will be taken even that little which they have. God requires only ten percent of our yield — beyond that is freewill offering. Should our government usurp more than that in the name of charity or humanitarian functions? Does government consider itself God, to know better than you what should be done by you with the fruits of your labor? Does government not agree with God that man should have free will to determine his own paths of destiny? Is government better than God, because God allows some to do without or suffer misfortune? What is the role of our nation under God? I tell you, God is a jealous God and His judgment will surely be upon that nation (or newspaper or individual) that tries to usurp His position by attempting to control men's minds and lives. This freedom of will, which God has given us, is an awesome freedom with great responsibilities — but He DOES NOT DICTATE TO US how we shall use it. Nor does He intend for government to dictate to us and control us. That government that spends the people's money with blatant irresponsibility, for no matter what cause, though it could be humanitarian, is usurping the freedom of individuals of generations to come. A slave can be defined as one who lacks economic freedom. This right of the individual is implicit in the Republican philosophy, and I pray it will not be destroyed by "equalizing the masses." Truly, that nation is governed best that is governed least; the only true function of government should be to protect us from enemies at home and abroad, and maintain a national stability for financial security and well-being.

In the last chapter of his book, J. Edgar Hoover tells us how to stay free. "Free man can learn here too; the truly revolutionary force of history is not material power but the spirit of religion... In communism we see what happens when freedom is extinguished. This must give us renewed zeal to work untiringly to uphold the ideals of justice and liberty which have made this nation great. With God's help, America will remain a land where people still know how to be free and brave."

Mrs. Lockerman, I'm enclosing an old article by J. Edgar Hoover in *Human Events*, which I know you think is partisan; but if you have faith in the FBI,

Mary M. O'Callaghan

please read this article and then, as a former member, write them for any current information or statistics about communism. Make it your duty to inform the nation, for much of this information has been suppressed by this Democratic Administration, which has proclaimed for itself a new right to the American people, the government's "RIGHT TO LIE." I urge you to use your position and every effort of your being to thwart this encroaching movement of communism. When I tried, you saw how eyebrows were raised accusingly, as if I were subversive or crazy, just as they have been raised against the John Birch Society, as if they were subversive. (No, I'm NOT a member!)

Please read also *Reader's Digest* articles "America, Wake Up," by Carlos P. Romulo (November 1960), "World War III Has Already Started," condensed by Max Eastman from *Protracted Conflict* (January 1961) and "The Insidious Campaign to Silence Anti-Communists," by William R. Kintner (May 1962). I will be glad to lend you my copies if you have none available. It is frightening what ground we have lost since these dates.

I am not trying to sway you to one candidate or one party, but perhaps you can better understand why people follow Goldwater almost religiously, because he is the ONLY candidate who recognizes the issue in the world today, which is that FREEDOM MUST BE PRESERVED. Creating bread-and-butter issues to cloud the vision of sincere and dedicated people to the real issue may be good politics, but it will surely lead our nation down the path of internal destruction. For me, this is not a fight to create or preserve a party or elect a candidate, but to serve my God in the fight for freedom and so to preserve His purposes in this world.

You say we do not understand the principles of the Good Samaritan because we oppose a poorly constructed (see your *Atlanta Journal* editorial) poverty bill. May I tell you a modern parable. "It was night in a large, bustling city. Lights were on in many apartments and TV's were entertaining the tired businessmen and wooing their wives to buy certain products because of certain claims when suddenly the night was pierced with shots, and a woman's screams of agony and cries for help split the outside darkness. Faces peered out of windows; shades were drawn; lights went out; but no one came. No one wanted to leave the safety of his home and involve himself in behalf of a stranger. Another shot, and there was silence — no more cries. The shades could go up; the TV's could go on again, because it was finished." Where was the Good Samaritan?

The Government Shall Be Upon Whose Shoulder?

"But", you say, "this isn't a parable; it actually happened!" It has happened over and over again, every time a free nation looked to America for help as it was being knifed and destroyed by godless Communism. And our fine, free Christian nation pulled down the shades until it was over, so we would not see the demise. "Such a tragedy," we sadly shook our heads, "but it was really none of our affair! And since we know the culprit, let's be smart and make friends, lest he turn to destroy us. Too bad he tortured and murdered and enslaved and stole; can we be blamed? Our shades were drawn and we really didn't see. What difference does it make if he ruthlessly controls twenty-five percent of the world's area and almost one billion people, so long as our home is barricaded and loaded with weapons, so he can't get in to hurt us? I'm sure he was just fooling when he said he'd bury us! Why, sure, we live side by side with him; it is comfortable to embrace peaceful coexistence. I am certainly not going to bother him. Who needs a Good Samaritan, anyway?"

I ask you, if the once-free men of this world cannot look to America for freedom, to whom can they look? To no one — only to God! Are we or are we not His emissaries?"

Patrick Henry's words would not have echoed down the years had he said, "Give me peace, or give me death!" Hear the entire quotation: "Is life so dear, or peace so sweet, as to be purchased at the price of chains and slavery? Forbid it, Almighty God! I know not what course others may take, but as for me, give me liberty, or give me death!"

I am no journalist, but this is my impassioned plea for genuine leadership from those of our elected officials, as well as from the public media, who hold the public trust. Dissolve the bread-and-butter issues in the heat of the fray for freedom on this Earth. Can you say that is not humanitarian? Perhaps the future of the nation is in your hands and in the hands of the rest of the public media. Look to God and serve Him well.

Sincerely,
Mary (Mrs. Jim) O'Callaghan

What's Happening to the Spirit of America?

This chapter is an address by Ed W. Hiles, who was Executive Vice President of the Georgia Savings and Loan League. The address was awarded the George Washington Gold Medal by the Freedoms Foundation of Valley Forge for its contribution to a better understanding of the American way of life. It is reproduced here in its totality:

Whenever I am fortunate enough to get this many people in a captive audience, I am tempted to take advantage of the situation and talk about the savings and loan business which I am privileged to represent. As a matter of fact, the subject which I have chosen is not altogether unrelated to our business of encouraging thrift and home ownership, and it is definitely something in which you and I and the savings and loan business have a common interest.

The slogan of our business is "The American Home — Safeguard of American Liberties." I want to devote my time with you today to the matter of our safeguarding of these liberties.

I have chosen as my topic the question "What's Happening to the Spirit of America?" I have done so purposely and not with any intent of trying to answer the question for you, but primarily for the purpose of impressing upon you the truth of the fact that something has been happening to the Spirit of America over the years, and I hope to leave you with your minds made up to do some real soul-searching in an effort to determine for yourself just what it is.

In referring to the "Spirit of America" I am talking about that spirit which is built upon and which evolves from the interrelationship of Christian morality and individual responsibility. To me, these are the basic components of the true Spirit of America, and it is my personal feeling that during the past three or four decades we have witnessed a gradual breaking down in the interrelationship of these two components to the extent that it poses a genuine threat to:

> Our freedom as individuals,
> The sanctity of our homes,
> The solvency of our businesses,

The Government Shall Be Upon Whose Shoulder?

> The stability of our economy,
> The integrity of our nation, and
> The peace of the world.

I recognize that this is an election year, and I am sure some of you are going to attempt to read into my comments implications of a political nature which certainly are not intended; however, let me say this — if it is true (and I believe it is true) that our individual freedoms are being sacrificed bit by bit on the altar of political expediency, then I firmly believe it is high time that we resorted to whatever political influences are available to us in order to recapture them.

But I am not here today as a politician, not as a Republican or as a Democrat or as a member of any of the much-discussed extremist groups. One thing which bothers me a great deal is the fact that today whenever a man gets on his feet to publicly endorse the philosophy of government that has made the United States of America the greatest nation on the face of the earth, he immediately is branded as an extremist. If being extremely concerned about what is happening to the Spirit of America makes me an extremist, then I will admit to being an extremist.

But I feel somewhat like the old man who had always loved to listen to a clock strike. He bought an old clock and hung it on the wall of his living room, and he would go to bed at night and listen to the clock strike. As the clock would strike, he would count. One night something went wrong with the mechanism in the clock. It began to strike, and he began to count. He got up to ten, eleven, twelve, thirteen, fourteen, fifteen — suddenly he realized something was wrong. He reached over, shook his wife and said, "Wake up Ma — it's later'n I've ever knowed it to be."

I feel as though it's later than a lot of us realize it to be — and so I want to talk with you, not as a politician nor as the Executive Vice-President of the Georgia Savings and Loan League, but as Ed Hile — a husband, father, professed Christian, and a fellow citizen of the United States of America.

This matter of individual freedom and Christian morality, as the basis for the true Spirit of America, has been of interest and concern to me for many years. But my decision to take a public stand on some of the issues involved was actually triggered by a very simple — yet significant — incident a few months ago.

Mary M. O'Callaghan

While attempting to assist with the coaching and organizing of a group of Little League beginners in baseball, I could not help but notice how much greater effort one of those little fellows would put forth when trying to win the right to play the position he wanted most to play on the team than when playing in a position assigned to him by his coach. Here was a very simple — yet very positive — example of how the exercise of freedom of choice was serving as the incentive for these boys to reach the very pinnacle of their individual abilities.

I found myself comparing this simple example with some of the results of the ever-changing concepts of the so-called American Way of Life in our time. I asked myself: Just how much honest-to-goodness freedom of choice is going to be available to these boys as an incentive to make the most of their individual lives when they get a few years older?

God has blessed my home with three wonderful children. But I shudder at the thought of the very real possibility that their futures are going to be determined for them — not through their individual choice, but as a result of our steady and positive drifting into a state of controlled lives; not under communism, but under a converted form of Americanism as envisioned by those who espouse the idea of exchanging freedom for security.

If this should actually happen — and we are most surely headed rapidly in that direction — it will be due largely to default on the part of our generation in allowing something to happen to the Spirit of America as based on Christian morality and individual freedom and responsibility.

I am taking my stand with those who believe that this is too big a price to pay for the type of security promised. History records that throughout all time, whenever people have decided they wanted security more than they wanted freedom, they have ended up losing both.

Two boys in England were watching some birds flying about the treetops above them. One of the boys asked the other why he was looking so sad. "I was thinking of those poor little birds up there," he said, "they haven't any cages."

He was sad because the birds were not safe in bondage like boys and men in a socialistic planned economy. He was born into — and was growing up under — that kind of philosophy. How about my Little League ball players?

The Government Shall Be Upon Whose Shoulder?

Remember, we actually started on our paternalistic binge some thirty years ago, when the hardships brought on by the Great Depression shortened that famous cry of Patrick Henry from "give me liberty or give me death" to just plain "give me."

We began to take liberties with the Ten Commandments similar to those which are being taken today with the Constitution of the United States of America. We began to twist our interpretation of the Ten Commandments in order to satisfy our immediate needs and desires or to justify our actions. We apparently changed our interpretation of the Tenth Commandment from "thou shalt not covet" to "thou shalt not covet except what thou would have from thy neighbor who owns it."

We began asking our government not only to protect us in what we had, but to give us a part of what someone else had. We failed to recognize that if we granted to the government the power to give us everything we wanted, we had to also give it the power to take from us everything we have.

We have followed this line pretty closely regardless of which political party happened to be in power in Washington. We have seen the tentacles of the octopus of federal aid and federal subsidy extending into virtually every phase of our economic, social and cultural life. And we have been swallowing the sugarcoated propaganda that we can have all this and freedom too.

But is this the same kind of freedom that our forefathers deemed worthy of such tremendous sacrifices as were made in the founding of this great nation of ours? I don't think so. I believe there is a difference — a great difference — between "freedom from something," which might be called protective freedom, and "freedom for something," or dynamic freedom, which serves to inspire man to strive to reach greater heights.

I am of the personal opinion that the finest statement yet made in referring to the court decision on prayer in the public schools was that made by evangelist Billy Graham. He said: "The trouble appears to be that a lot of people are of the opinion that the Constitution grants them freedom FROM religion instead of freedom OF religion..."

We, as a people, have consistently over the past three decades sought freedom from individual responsibilities by either asking or simply allowing the Federal Government to assume more and more of such responsibilities without any objection on our part.

Mary M. O'Callaghan

It is this trend toward "protective freedom," or "freedom from something," which, in my opinion, is eating away at the Spirit of America.

So my hope today is that you will think along with me while we attempt to establish the four cornerstones of the foundation of true freedom as envisioned by our forefathers.

First of all, we are well aware of the great conflict which exists today between two basic ideologies of government — one based on freedom, the other on enslavement. We have heard and read many lengthy discussions attempting to set forth the differences between these two systems. But if I were asked to write a book on the subject, it would probably be the shortest book ever written. I would have an artist prepare an attractive cover setting out the title in bold letters: ***THE REAL DIFFERENCE BETWEEN AMERICANISM AND COMMUNISM***. Inside there would be just one page, and on that page one word. The word would be **G O D** in capital letters.

Our nation became a great nation because it was a good nation. Whenever it ceases to be a good nation, it will cease to be a great nation.

We in America take great pride, and rightly so, in the fact that we enjoy the highest standard of living of any people on the face of the earth. We take great pride, and rightly so, in the tremendous material wealth of this country. We take great pride, and rightly so, in the tremendous productive capacity of this country. We take great pride in, and place great reliance upon, the tremendous military might of this country. These things are important, but in placing a measure of value on the importance of these things, we must not lose sight of the truth of the fact that our ultimate salvation as free individuals is going to depend not on these things we have in our hands, but on what we have in our hearts.

So the First Cornerstone of Freedom, so far as I am concerned, must of necessity be a basic, fundamental belief in — and reliance upon — an Almighty God. This cornerstone was set by the signers of the Declaration of Independence when they wrote into that great document these words: "We hold these truths to be self-evident ... that all men are endowed by their Creator with certain inalienable rights, that among these are life, liberty, and the pursuit of happiness."

They firmly believed that these rights came from God — not from government. Our own belief today should be just as genuine and not the "lip service" type of belief which exists in so many quarters. We stamp our coins with the words, "In God we trust" — and then we cast

The Government Shall Be Upon Whose Shoulder?

our lot and our loyalties, sometimes blindly, with some political party or group espousing an ideology which time and again, throughout history, has led other nations to disaster.

Sometimes I wonder if we aren't unwittingly breaking the First Commandment by getting ourselves in the position of making a god of government and forgetting about the government of God.

It has been suggested that we are rewriting the twenty-third Psalm so that it would read:

> The government is my shepherd; I shall not work.
> It maketh me to lie down in a fool's paradise,
> It leadeth me into deep water,
> But it refills my dinner pail.

Is this what's happening to the Spirit of America?

The Second Cornerstone of Freedom is a government limited by Constitution.

We know that government is necessary and that it costs money. But whatever degree of government we have, it must be the servant and not the master of the people. That was clearly the intent of the framers of our Constitution.

They had learned from experience that the gravest and most constant danger to a man's life, liberty and happiness is the government under which he lives.

They were not only students of history — they were victims of it.

They had no federal subsidy — nor did they seek any. All they had was character. All they did was work. All they wanted was self-respect.

They earned through sacrifice what we have been privileged to enjoy through heritage and what is now being dissipated by our complacency. To make certain we would never have to suffer the tyranny from which they had fled, they wrote into the Constitution three unique characteristics:

1. The authority of the government was limited to specific delegated powers.
2. All authority or power not so delegated remained with the states or the people.
3. The power of government was divided into three separate branches with specific duties and realms of influence.

Mary M. O'Callaghan

This was a written contract between the government and the people. It wasn't intended to be made flexible or amended by court interpretations in order to comply with some expressed policy of whatever political party happened to be in power.

This was no doubt the greatest governmental document ever struck by the pen of man. And as it has been handed down from generation to generation, it has carried with it some very definite responsibilities for its preservation and protection on the part of those for whom its benefits were intended — the people of the United States of America. On leaving the Convention Hall when the final draft had been agreed upon, Ben Franklin was approached by a citizen with this question: "Dr. Franklin, what have you given us?" He replied: "We have given you a Republic — if you can keep it." He didn't say, "If the President can keep it." He didn't say, "If the Congress can keep it." He said to that citizen, "If YOU can keep it."

But somehow, when we changed Patrick Henry's cry to "give me," we either lost sight of — or deliberately turned our backs on — Ben Franklin's challenge.

With the help of a few government planners, we developed a new game of "ring-around-a-rosy." In it we all stand in a circle, each with his hand in the pocket of the person next to him expecting to get richer therefrom. We still seem to be blind to the truth of the fact that whenever a man gets something without earning it, someone else must earn something without getting it. That is morally wrong, and any society building upon such a foundation is bound to crumble.

We hear a lot of talk about federal aid. To me this is a misnomer. There is no such thing as federal aid. In fact, the thing which we refer to as federal aid can only be obtained in two ways.

The first way is for the government to take something from us in order to have it to give back to us. That is ridiculous, and to me it is like a person giving himself a blood transfusion by taking the blood from the right arm and inserting it in the left arm — meanwhile running it through a tube that leaks. Under this system we would soon find ourselves in the position cited in the legend about the wolves in the Arctic Region, who are tricked into capture by the Eskimos.

The Eskimos embed a sharp knife in the ice, with only a small portion of a razor-sharp point of the blade protruding. Around this blade they pour a small quantity of seal blood. The wolves, attracted by the blood, begin to lap at it and soon find that the faster they lap up the blood, the more blood appears. They become so overwhelmed with this apparently inexhaustible supply of blood that they continue to lap at it until they grow so weak from loss of their own blood that they fall over on the ice and freeze to death.

Is that what is happening to the Spirit of America?

The other way in which we can receive this so-called federal aid is for the government to take it from someone else in order to give it to us. If we removed the government from this operation, it would become a direct violation of the Eighth Commandment — "Thou shalt not steal" — unless, of course, we wanted to "amend" this one to read, "Thou shalt not steal — except for a worthy cause."

I think it is unfortunate today that even our churches, which are supposedly the custodians of the Ten Commandments, not only are condoning but are actually demanding by their active and aggressive support of do-good welfare-type legislation that the fruits of the labor of some citizens be taken by force of law for the benefit of other citizens. To me this is an admission of failure on the part of the churches in their rightful area of persuasion and influence, and effort to substitute compulsion.

Is this a result of, or a contributing factor to what is happening to the Spirit of America?

The Third Cornerstone of Freedom is Christian ethics.

If something is morally wrong, I do not believe it can be made morally right simply by passing a law making it legal. By the same token, if something is not morally wrong, it can't be made so merely by passing a law making it illegal. This is basic to some of the problems confronting us as a Christian nation today.

The criteria for right or wrong come from sources outside the government, and they existed long before any current government was formalized.

I am going to attempt to draw for you an extreme analogy and I will admit to its extremeness, but I am hopeful that it will help to make a point. All of you have read during recent months about a young fellow by the name of Billie Sol Estes. Let's remember that when we started on our paternalistic binge in this country some three and a half decades ago, Billie Sol Estes had not yet begun his first grade education. He was born into and grew up in an era and an area where one group of citizens was collecting money from another group of citizens for not planting cotton, for not planting corn, and for not producing pigs; and what is

Mary M. O'Callaghan

Billie Sol Estes being sent to prison for? He is being sent to prison for collecting money from farmers for not producing fertilizer tanks. Here are two operations similar in nature, both of which are morally wrong because each consists of one person getting something without earning it, thereby making another person earn something without getting it. One is sending a man to prison; the other is perfectly right and legal in the eyes of the law.

Let's take a close look at the Christian ethics of this philosophy of federal aid, of the subsidizing of one segment of our economy at the expense of another. Do we honestly believe it is morally right for the government to say to us: "We will protect you from being robbed on one hand; but if you can demonstrate the need, we will arrange for others to be robbed in your behalf"?

What sort of progress are we making in America when we urge our elected officials, by resolution and otherwise, to pass laws which will destroy human dignity by making half of the people victims of piracy and the other half victims of charity?

Please understand that I am not against charity. But it has always been my personal belief that charity, in order to be effective, must be voluntary. I refer briefly to the thirteenth and fourteenth verses of the twelfth chapter of the book of Luke from the New Testament. Jesus was talking to a large crowd when a man approached him saying: *"Master, speak to my brother, that he divide the inheritance with me."* To this Jesus replied: *"Man, who made me a judge or a divider over you?"*

The Fourth Cornerstone of Freedom is found in the individual strength of character among our people themselves.

It is my feeling that we have been witnessing a tremendous amount of erosion at this cornerstone of the Foundation of Freedom. This erosion has reached a point where we now find ourselves entrapped in a tremendous web of inconsistencies. Somehow we must generate the strength of character to throw off these inconsistencies one by one if we are going to recapture or reestablish the true Spirit of America.

For example, we are trapped in an inconsistency between what we truly believe and what we do. This is personal and individual, and it consists primarily of giving our consciences a little bigger voice in the making of our decisions.

We are trapped in an inconsistency between our true political philosophies and our traditions of blind loyalty to political parties. As far as I am personally concerned, I have no special preference as to whether

The Government Shall Be Upon Whose Shoulder?

my children grow up under a Democratic Republic or a Republican Democracy, but I do not want to see them grow up under a politically amalgamated autocracy.

We are trapped in an inconsistency between our desire to have government take from others and give to us, and our objections to having the government take from us and give to others.

Between our demands for freedom from government control of our respective businesses and our failure at or refusal of self-regulation.

Between our desire for less government and our rejection of more individual responsibilities.

Between the enactment of laws purported to guarantee opportunity to succeed and the application and enforcement of those laws in such a way as to destroy the incentive to succeed.

Between court decisions purported to protect human rights and the application and enforcement of those decisions in such a way as to destroy property rights.

Between court opinions purported to grant freedom of choice to a buyer and the application of those decisions in such a way as to deny the freedom of choice to a seller.

Between court decisions purported to guarantee freedom to associate and the application and enforcement of those decisions in such a way as to deny the freedom not to associate.

Between the enactment of a law under the title of so-called Civil Rights purported to guarantee freedom "from" discrimination and the application of that law in such a way as to compel discrimination by destroying freedom of choice.

Last, but not least, the inconsistency between a pledge of allegiance which contains the words "one nation under God" and court-written laws which deny to that God admittance to the classrooms of our children. These are just a few of the hundreds of inconsistencies in which we find ourselves entrapped. I am inclined to attribute our predicament:

>Not to our action, but to our inaction;
>Not to our choice, but to our surrender of choice to somebody else;
>Not to our desire to follow, but to our failure to lead;
>Not to our inability to prevent it, but to our indifference towards it;
>Not to our failure to recognize the threat, but to our refusal to admit its imminence.

Mary M. O'Callaghan

And so this cornerstone of strength of character is extremely important because freedom and character will rise and fall together — and freedom cannot long endure where there is no character to sustain it. Freedom is a precious thing. It is a God-given thing; it is a voluntary thing. But freedom is not free, and it must not be taken for granted. It was won through sacrifice, and it must be maintained through sacrifice wherever necessary. It can be lost just as surely, just as completely — and just as permanently — tax by tax, subsidy by subsidy, and regulation by regulation as it can be bullet by bullet, bomb by bomb, or missile by missile.

And so there you have one man's view of the basic foundation of freedom. It is my feeling that we are witnessing a steady decline of freedom in America. But it is not too late to stem the tide. You can be sure it will take strength of character of individual citizens. It will take a firm application of Christian ethics in the conduct of our relations with each other. It will take the restoration of constitutional limitations upon government. And it will also take one thing more.

At a critical period in biblical history when Joshua was chosen to lead the children of Israel into the land of Canaan, he said to his people, *"Choose you this day whom ye will serve ... but as for me and my house, we will serve the LORD"* (Joshua 24:15).

Some years ago there was discovered an epitaph on a tombstone along the coast of Greece. It read: "A shipwrecked sailor on this coast bids you set sail — full many a ship, ere we were lost, weathered the gale."

Still more recently in the news was a forty-five-year-old Marine Colonel responding to a question about his upcoming space attempt. He said to the people of America: "Some men will die — but keep on striving for your goal."

These three men lived centuries apart, but they had one thing in common: They had faith. They had faith in themselves. They had faith in their fellowmen. They had faith in their purpose. And above all, they had faith in God.

Real faith such as this is a living, vital force — and a constant source of strength and comfort.

The very faith that freedom will survive will, in itself, help freedom to survive. But we must never stop working at it if we are to recapture the true Spirit of America.

The Government Shall Be Upon Whose Shoulder?

To make our work most effective, then, we must stand on the first cornerstone we mentioned — a fundamental belief in and reliance upon God. We must ask Him to grant us the willingness to accept those things in our lives which cannot be changed. We must seek from Him the courage to change those things which can and must be changed. And we must look to Him for the wisdom to know the difference.

Author's note: May this be a tribute to the late Ed W. Hiles, extending his godly, patriotic fervor to this present generation for "…he being dead yet speaketh" (Hebrews 11:4b).

Merry Christmas Newsletter — 1964

Hey, it's Christmas again! The fragrance of Christmas trees and fresh greenery fills the house to tickle the memories of past happy holidays; brownies, cookies, popcorn and coffee cake scent the house with holiday incense; the jingling sounds of bells and music boxes mingle with the slightly off-key Salvation Army band, and choirs and carolers burst with the rapturous message of the birth of our Lord; tree lights twinkle, candles glow and stars beam in the crisp atmosphere to hail Him King; gifts of love are wrapped in gay paper by loving hands and stacked under the tree for those most exciting moments of childhood years; mistletoe sprigs whisper sly invitations; families hold hands across the miles and the years, and eyes grow moist and spill over with remembered blessings shared; and each Christmas card written and received is a bit of the heaven imparted to us at the birth of Christ. Friends and loved ones give meaning to this message of love poured forth almost two thousand years ago, and the O'Callaghans glow with the warmth of this sharing!

Nineteen sixty-four has been another happy, hectic and, fortunately, healthful year for us. Marky graduated from Emory in March and entered the business world of banking. In June she took an apartment with three friends to live in air-conditioned luxury. In rapid succession, she left the desk job, took a high school teaching job, learned the financial facts of life away from home, and moved back this week!

Jimbo returned to Emory this fall as a junior, armed with paint and rollers to spruce up the K.A. House where he resides.

Karen is enjoying the mad, mad whirl of her senior year in high school and is undergoing the dilemma of where to go from here. She is coeditor of her annual and officer of several clubs, and still strums her guitar and sings with a couple of groups. She thinks she might be interested in architecture, so save all of your houses and buildings for her to design!

Cindy is a sophomore, suffering from the politically caused frustrations of an unused learner's driving permit, which I must rectify the first of the year.

Wendy is now a real Girl Scout in the fourth grade, and Laurie is a real Brownie in the second. They took off with me and Mom O'Callaghan and Aunt "Ceal" again this year for our annual spring trek to Florida. We spent most of

The Government Shall Be Upon Whose Shoulder?

our time at Naples this year and saw everything from the Seminoles to seashells at Sanibel. We couldn't stay long because Wendy was nervous about goofing off from school.

Jim had business in Los Angeles this summer, so we flew there for a couple of days at the Beverly Hilton in Beverly Hills before proceeding to San Francisco via Las Vegas, to sit in on the National Republican Convention. The shows and food were good at Las Vegas, but the two days were sufficient for our lifetimes! You can imagine the thrill I experienced returning to Frisco for the first time since I had lived there at the age of eleven. From the Top of the Mark I thrilled to see the city my Dad thought was like Heaven on Earth. (That was in 1931!) I pretended that the ferryboat now anchored as a museum was once again riding across the bay, with the wind whipping my hair and the seagulls screaming as we chugged past the now unoccupied Alcatraz. The bright red Golden Gate Bridge peeping through the fog had made my ferryboats obsolete, and was new to me. Chinatown, Market Street, Fisherman's Wharf, cable cars, steep hills, and our old apartment on Sutter Street, only two blocks from the hotel where we were staying, all brought back fond memories of the time when I had first been a Girl Scout there!

My first National Republican Convention was thrilling, but you'd hardly recognize it from some of the reporting we heard about and read. It was interesting to watch the obviously unbathed and unkempt CORE kooks parading and chanting, "Jim Crow's got to go." I was amused when a young serviceman near me finally got up the courage to ask a policeman, "Who is Jim Crow?" And later, to no one in particular he added, "I'm from the South and I've never seen anything like this before!"

After the Convention we rented a car, crossed the Golden Gate Bridge, drove through the little artist colony village of Sausalito hugging the hills down to the waterfront, past Mt. Tamalpais, and on to Muir Woods, where we gloried in the magnificence of the giant redwoods, some of which may even have existed when the heavenly chorus proclaimed Christ's birth! Since this was government property, we dared not even pick up a fallen leaf, but a ranger crushed a bay leaf to let us sniff the aromatic fragrance! We drove on mountainous roads that fairly jutted out over the pounding Pacific that was way below us. We frolicked on the beach where Sir Francis Drake had landed, dabbling our toes in the chilly water. We located a marvelous little inn in a sleepy village run by a former

Mary M. O'Callaghan

Czech government minister who had escaped from his homeland on a moment's notice with only his family and family Bible. Their write-up was a true Republican story of opportunity and the success of hard work unhampered by wages and hours, and government fetters that are becoming more and more binding.

When we returned home, five days before the deadline for qualifying, only one young, unknown newcomer to Atlanta was in the race for Republican Fifth District Congressman. When Jim couldn't persuade any of the other logical prospects to take the plunge, there was no other choice but to put our $750 on the line, roll up our sleeves and get to work once again. There was much feeling and much hard work by many dedicated people in our campaign for the principles we espoused — the free enterprise system, limited government and constitutional government. Thank heavens for the new *Atlanta Times*, which gave us brief respites from the carving up and distortions we suffered at the hands of the *Atlanta Constitution* and *Journal*. We got an unprecedented high of sixty-five percent of the white vote, but that was not enough to overcome a forty-thousand-bloc vote. They even distorted our returns on election night, to broadcast to the West Coast where they were still voting. We're glad it's over and particularly glad Georgia finally went Republican one time!

We've had a nice vacation in Florida and will still fight for what we believe in, but right now we believe in a Merry Christmas and Happy New Year for all!

The Jim O'Callaghan Clan

Commentary — 1998 on the '64 Elections

The 1962 Georgia Fifth Congressional District had been gerrymandered for the 1964 elections to exclude Emory and Decatur so that Emory University (Methodist), Columbia Theological Seminary (Presbyterian) and Agnes Scott College were no longer in our district. Forty-three clergymen and professors of Christianity from these three prestigious institutes signed a published petition decrying the intrusion of "religion into politics," thus opposing the Becker Amendment, which simply gave local citizens the right to choose concerning prayer in schools. Obviously the aim of these forty-three educators was to make a blanket endorsement for their Democratic candidate, which they could not do publicly. By supporting his negative stand on this important issue, they did elect their Democratic candidate, but denied the God of Abraham, Isaac and Jacob access to the American schoolchildren.

Since these educators were no longer in the Fifth District, it was not political motivation that prompted Mary to take time from the busy campaign (to say nothing of scheduling six children) to mail each of these forty-three theologians a letter. It was prompted by the shock and dismay that any teacher of the Gospel would deny the very foundation of the nation, a freedom enjoyed for almost two hundred years! Who was the enemy anyway? Though the 1964 voters did send Democrats to Congress from these two districts, for the first time since reconstruction days, Georgia did support the Republican Presidential nominee, Goldwater!

Thirty-four years later, 1998, the right to have prayer, Bible reading and the Ten Commandments displayed in our public schools remains an embattled issue. God is systematically being purged from all American life, including our courtrooms. For years now, ungodly leaders and an ungodly press have spewed their left-wing propaganda to intimidate and inoculate an unsuspecting populace. Many Christians, ignorant of their authority and rights, and not willing to get into the fray, have accepted this loss of freedom as proper and inevitable.

Contrary to biblical injunctions, some denominational governing bodies have accepted or debated lesbian and homosexual ordinations among their clergy. Such a debate is tantamount to an open denial of the truth and the authority of God's Word in the church! It is heartbreaking to watch these denominations slowly but meticulously commit suicide by deliberate overdoses of secular humanistic poison!

Mary M. O'Callaghan

The innocent blood of millions of aborted babies has been shed in our land, and the same people who are horrified to read in their Bibles about child sacrifices to Molech have not demanded and have not required a change in American philosophy and actions. What do they call this modern god? "Convenience." Or do they prefer "Political Correctness"? Why is there not a thunderous outcry from our leaders and from the press against the horrifying murder, planned and agreed to by parents and practitioners for a sum of money, to stab children and suck their brains out before they are born or even in the process of being born? It seems that every choice is legally protected, including the murder of the innocent, but those pertaining to biblical standards. God forbid! We have sown the wind and are reaping the whirlwind!

Why are we shocked at the violence in our schools as children murder classmates and teachers in these schools where we have denied God an entrance? Why are we surprised at the drugs and violence in our society where God has been eliminated from every aspect of public American life? Why have we embraced foreign and pagan gods that have been imported into our land, and yet have denied the God of Abraham, Isaac and Jacob upon whom this nation was founded and who is proclaimed on every penny, nickel, dime, and quarter — every coin and even every printed piece of currency — "IN GOD WE TRUST"? Will someone please name this god if He is not the God of the Bible?

We have required God to step aside in favor of a few atheists and the ACLU, misnamed the "American Civil Liberties Union." It is certainly not American in the traditional sense. It is not even civil! And it does not promote liberty. But it is a very powerful, ungodly union, dedicated to the legal attack of everything pertaining to God. In short, it is satanic and demonic, preprogrammed to deceive and destroy. It must be the people's choice or else they would rise up and outlaw it! In America, our opinions are expressed at the ballot box. We have knowingly elected and reelected ungodly, immoral and amoral, unrepentant, degenerate, lying candidates to lead our nation, obliviously unaware they are taking us with them straight to hell!

THE WATER IS GETTING HOTTER! IS IT TOO LATE TO JUMP?

A second letter went forth in January from Mary to the amazing forty-three clergymen who united to deny God an entrance into our public schools. May God grant them repentance!

Post-election Letter to Forty-three Atlanta Area Clergymen and Educators

January 8, 1965

Dear Christian Leader,

Since many of you ministers and teachers were kind enough not only to read my pre-election letter, hastily dictated over the phone, but also to honor me with a reply, I hope you will indulge me with a few more minutes of your time.

First of all, let me agree that it is a good old American custom that we do not all have to agree, and had you simply as individuals publicly endorsed your chosen candidate, which is any private citizen's privilege, you wouldn't be bothered with me. But I have yet to get over the shock of educators from our two great theological seminaries, and college, uniting to publicly oppose the Becker Amendment. That amendment will not in any way whatsoever change or weaken the First Amendment to our Constitution but seeks to restore the inherent American right to the "free exercise" of religion as guaranteed by it and then denied by Supreme Court rulings. This amendment, House Joint Resolution 693, was authored by a committee of six Congressmen, three each Democratic and Republican, appointed by more than sixty House members who had introduced similar resolutions and wished to arrive at one text acceptable to all, with the aid of constitutional lawyers and legislative counsel. Congressman Becker introduced it, and rather than seek reelection, he devoted full time to bringing the message before the people. He said, "I cannot sit idly by and permit the advocates of a godless society to accomplish in the U.S. what the Communists have accomplished in Russia."

Please do not misunderstand me that I think I am wiser or more pious or more dedicated to God than any of you; far from it. But I take courage to write you, remembering that Christ said we must all come as little children. When I urged you to wake up and proclaim God broadly and unashamedly I was not trying to accuse you of being derelict in your job, but in a bumbling way was trying to exhort you to "claim" Him as ours, in every phase of our lives.

God is not God just on Sunday, but is always ever-present, omniscient and almighty, Lord of lords, and King of kings, and even President of presidents! The purpose of our lives, as well as the purpose of our state and education, is to glorify Him, the Creator of all. Either God is God or He isn't, or we really don't know. Theism, atheism and agnosticism are all religions, so that if we refuse to allow God to be honored in our schools we are establishing atheism or agnosticism as our state religion. God is a jealous God and will have no other gods before Him, including secular humanists playing God. As long as He has been the cornerstone of our country and we have built our government on God-given principles and rights, and so recognized them as proceeding from God, our nation has been blessed.

If then you agree that God is the author of all power and authority, can you vote to deny Him daily worship by the children of America, who for many years have been unapologetically so nurtured? Can you honestly face the prospect of standing before your Maker and saying, "But God, we had to be fair to those other folks who don't believe in You, and give them their turn. You did want us to be fair, didn't You, God? After all, we all have doubts on occasions; and besides, I don't want my Presbyterian children participating in those Baptist prayers (forgetting that that has been done for years now)! You do understand, don't You, God? It is enough that we adults remember You on civic occasions, isn't it, and children really don't get anything out of those few verses and prayers mumbled, so we didn't think it was important for our children to honor and worship You in all phases of their lives. Individual teachers might simply confuse them, so we left You out of our schools, God, considering it immaterial, irrelevant, and perhaps even irreverent. You do understand, don't You, God?"

And WILL God understand? Will the God who has commissioned us to be His witnesses to all creation, and the God to whom we profess all homage and honor for all creation, including states and schools, understand? Or is this "God bit" mere hokum, since the atheists of this world are far more dedicated to their pronouncements than the godly are? God simply does not leave room for any other religion. As a Christian nation, serving the God of Abraham, Isaac and Jacob through Jesus the Messiah, we have been blessed like a second Promised Land, flowing with milk and honey and opportunity! But like the old Israel, when we leave God out and rely on our own strength and wisdom, we are doomed as a nation. What folly to believe "in" God and not believe God!

Surely I am not the only one among you who is willing to fight for the privilege of honoring God in our schools. With every child that is baptized in my

The Government Shall Be Upon Whose Shoulder?

church I take the vow with the rest of the congregation to help rear that child in the nurture and admonition of the Lord. I can do this on weekdays as well as on Sunday by continuing to fight to give God a place of honor in all of life, especially in the vital learning processes. Why am I going to this trouble in a day when we no longer even expect people to take vows seriously? Because I discovered long ago the most precious heritage I can leave my six children is a strong faith in a loving, unchanging and just God, and that is not a gift from me but from God. I must try to be the good steward. I want that heritage not just for my children but for all children because it is precious and what makes life whole. Certainly you can educate without God, but what have you got when you do? I don't care to live in that kind of society. God must be in mathematics, and science, and geography and history, for the truth is not taught where He is excluded.

Since writing you forty-three clergymen and educators of the Gospel of Jesus Christ my previous pre-election letter, the Holy Spirit strangely led me to two pieces of publication that make me know I am being directed. I took my children to the library with no thought of reading, myself, during this pre-Christmas rush. I went immediately to a counter of current books, which I have never previously perused, and my eye fell on one book alone, *The Supreme Court and Public Prayer*, by Dr. Charles E. Rice, Associate Professor of Law at Fordham University. I urge you to examine this book even if you have time for only the preface and a chapter or two. It speaks so eloquently the things that I am stumbling to say, and traces throughout our nation's history the presupposition that God is our God and we never intended to separate Him from our state affairs, though our church governments are separate from our national government.

The other publication is the *Columbia Theological Seminary Quarterly*, April 1964. At this busy time there was nothing on the cover to excite me to open and examine this particular volume, among my many other magazines, but I was somehow compelled to. On page one was the title "God and the State: a Plea for Prayer in the Schools" under the foreword, "This article represents research done by Dr. William C. Robinson under an assignment of the Permanent Theological Committee of the General Assembly of the Presbyterian Church, U.S...."

I realize a word from me bears little weight with you, for I have no claims to authority, but I commend to you this carefully researched paper. On page twenty-four, Dr. Robinson exhorts that "the Christian acting as a citizen should use every proper method to continue the recognition of God in the public schools." This Jim

Mary M. O'Callaghan

and I have tried to do by first offering for public office, pledged to this legislation, and now as private citizens, branded extremists by our local press for these efforts.

I can't help but point out what is happening in Washington while I am thus occupied. Your old and new Congressmen have invited your declared mortal enemy, the enemy of God Almighty, to visit and sup at our table, to spread his propaganda over our own TV, to share our secrets through laxity and corruption in high places, and to seduce us to completely disarm ourselves. (If you write for a copy of Department of State Publication 7277, released in September 1961, you will be told it is out of print, for this U.S. disarmament program is not what the American people are supposed to ponder. Ralph McGill, editor of the *Atlanta Constitution*, is on one of the disarmament committees and could fill you in on how fast McNamara is proceeding to disarm us, though we are currently engaged in world conflict even if we won't admit it. And Cuba sits ninety miles off our coast using thousands of tons of concrete, though no new building above ground is in evidence.) Where can we call for help when this enemy starts to bury us, as he has vowed to do, and have our children brought up under godless communism — a more advanced phase of socialism? It was said America would never wittingly adopt socialism, but under the guise of "liberalism" we would choose it. The Russians have said communism will be our OWN choice.

My friends, when the positions of conservatives and patriots are given dirty connotations, it is time to beware. The conservative seeks only to preserve constitutional government as originally conceived, with the checks and balances that have made our country great and unique in the world. It has nothing to do with race; but it does require limited government, for government has always been the chief usurper of personal freedoms.

May I ask those of you who may be supporting our mushrooming welfare state to consider ten "cannots" gleaned from the writings and speeches of Abraham Lincoln, which I hold as irrefutable truths.

"You cannot bring about prosperity by discouraging thrift."
"You cannot help small men by tearing down big men."
"You cannot strengthen the weak by weakening the strong."
"You cannot lift the wage earner by pulling down the wage payer."
"You cannot help the poor man by destroying the rich."

The Government Shall Be Upon Whose Shoulder?

"You cannot keep out of trouble by spending more than your income."
"You cannot further the brotherhood of man by inciting class hatred."
"You cannot establish security on borrowed money."
"You cannot build character and courage by taking away man's initiative and independence."
"You cannot help men permanently by doing for them what they could do for themselves."

Some of you may support Medicare without realizing the present multi-billion dollar indebtedness of Social Security. This is not a funded insurance, as required by law for private business, but a tax that goes into and out of the big melting pot. Georgia, along with every other state, has already adopted the Kerr-Mills Act, which will adequately take care of the medical needs of all the needy, not just the aged, including those who have some income but would be impoverished by lengthy illness. When asked why he has not requested that this bill be fully implemented in Georgia, Governor Sanders says out of one side of his mouth that Georgia does not have the money, and out of the other side of his mouth he brags of our prosperity. May I suggest to you that our Negro citizens, where the needs are greatest, would benefit mostly by this bill; and he is unwilling to spend our Georgia money for these Georgia citizens.

In this last election, including our own (though I hope we were not, nor will ever be party to such), I witnessed such distressing distortion of the truth to make me realize that manipulation of people is the current goal, not honest statesmanship and competition; it was as if the ends justify the means. Our opponent told the Negro community that their cause would be set back twenty years if they elected a conservative and they had better get out the vote and elect him. Jim was told by Negro leaders that he could get some of their vote if he would repudiate Goldwater and the principles of constitutionality upon which they both stand. That price of compromise would have been too dear for him personally and for the country.

Dr. McDowell Richards (President of Columbia Theological Seminary), who was asked but declined to sign your anti-Becker Amendment statement, reminds me that essentially the mission of the Church must be spiritual, and I go further and say that the spiritual must not be left out of education and government. I urge you, as individual citizens, to actively participate in government and politics, diligently searching for the truth, a vital necessity under an administration admit-

Mary M. O'Callaghan

tedly following a "right to lie" policy. God has been, and will always be, involved with authority, so don't deplore His being intruded into politics; rather, make the Church relevant by working for and insisting on His will in all matters and decisions, and our country may yet be saved. Though there may be some elements of good to a Great Society, I challenge it as blasphemous. Dare one man set up his state or himself as being all things to all people? God alone has created the "great society" and called it the Church; had those of us who belong been more faithful to it and God's principles, our country might not now be on the verge of moral and financial bankruptcy.

Thank you for patiently hearing me through. My prayers are with you as we start this new year in the service of the Lord not that you will see my way, but that we will all see God's way.

Sincerely,
Mary O'Callaghan

P.S. Only today, in the *Atlanta Constitution*, do we find admission of impending bankruptcy, couched in the same semantics that have made of the word "patriot" something less than desirable, and of those who would fight communism "extremists," "Birchites," or "McCarthyites." You have to search for it on page forty-three, under a headline that makes us sound very secure, then incidentally it mentions that President Johnson considers eliminating the gold backing for part of the U.S. money supply. A theory that this may really be a boon is dished up for you to swallow, and "gold hoarders" seem to be the only ones finding weakness therein. The facts: U.S. gold stocks in 1964 were at fifteen billion dollars. Foreign countries can redeem aid dollars for gold. U.S. citizens cannot. Due bills held by foreign nations total twenty-four billion dollars, so they could bankrupt the U.S. Treasury. At present, law requires that eleven billion dollars be on hand for the backing of forty-five billion in U.S. currency, the law Johnson speaks of changing. To date we have paid out one hundred four billion in foreign aid to one hundred nations, many voting consistently against us in the U.N., plus one and six-tenths billion dollars in U.S. food shipments. As an example, Sukarno has received eight hundred million dollars of it! Three and three-tenths billion dollars is the amount of 1965 foreign aid passed by the House. France has now demanded gold payment on one hundred fifty million dollars in notes. Is this just the

The Government Shall Be Upon Whose Shoulder?

beginning, or will it stop here? Our national debt ceiling of three hundred twenty-four billion is more than the combined debt of all other nations of the world, and our budget doesn't show all the spending. In the past ten years, budget spending has gone up fifty-one percent and cash spending seventy-three. In times supposed to be prosperous, since 1960, thirty-one billion dollars have been added to the national debt, six billion dollars in fiscal 1964 despite LBJ's talk of economy. Our national debt is actually estimated in the trillions! William Stringfellow castigated Goldwater as following the old religion of materialism, even though his elected duty would have been to concern himself with these facts and figures and the material welfare of American citizens. Should a minister be concerned for fiscal responsibility? Should a mother? Should a father? Should a Christian? Why are we deceiving ourselves? Our salvation is in a return to God and the truth.

Commentary — 1998 and Two Letters from 1965

As I review and copy these words and facts from American life in the 1960s, I am appalled at the progress that has been made toward the destruction of America, as we have known it! I do not recall which of the Russian Communist leaders was the honored guest of America at the time of this original report, but I do know that Gorbachev is currently headquartered in the Presidio in San Francisco, and has been for some time. I have never heard a cancellation of the Communist threat to bury us, with or without the Iron Curtain! It seems as if we are supplying our various enemies with our own tools to destroy us! They boasted we would even vote for it ourselves! Will we? Have we?

HOW HOT IS THE WATER NOW? HOW HIGH CAN WE JUMP?

Whether it be a Great Society, or a one world government, or a New World Order, or the current code word, "Global Village," it all spells out Mystery Babylon, Babylon the Great! We have been stretching towards the culmination of the ages; but now time is speeding up, the circumstances are lining up, the players are getting in position, and the means have been prepared for the climax of prophecy!

Are you looking up? Our redemption is drawing nigh!

The following letter is addressed to a journalist friend, name changed, who campaigned for Jim's Democratic opponent in the 1962 and 1964 Fifth Congressional District races, Atlanta, Georgia. Charles Weltner won in 1962 and was therefore incumbent in 1964.

Atlanta, Georgia
January 6, 1965

Dear Joe,

Christmas decorations are put away and holiday activities have ceased so I can now take time to answer your nice and thoughtful letter.

The Government Shall Be Upon Whose Shoulder?

The initial falsification of our campaign results announced across the nation (1998 note — Western states were still voting and only after midnight was a large number of "missing" votes found and recorded) was just another indication of the rottenness which we were trying to fight. When the correct results were quietly given at a late, late, late hour; we knew that the moral victory was ours, for we polled sixty-five percent of the white vote. We knew we could not beat a forty-thousand-bloc vote that didn't honestly know what it was voting for, since facts don't seem to be very popular or pertinent these days, from the national Administration down. The popular thing now is to manipulate, and the ends seem to justify any means. This includes your friend Weltner, and Eugene Patterson and his Atlanta Newspapers, Inc., who seek to play God with people's minds, dishing out what they want them to hear, and distorting it where they please. I have more respect for the prostitute in the street than for this kind of intellectual prostitution, hiding behind an honorable front.

How can you respect an able-bodied man who, after all danger of Korea has passed, goes on active duty with the armed forces for his stated purpose of having it appear on his record when he seeks a political career! I nearly choked when Weltner was introduced as a Veteran — an insult to every man who has given himself selflessly to the service of his country. (1998 note — Jim retired as a Colonel, Air Force Reserves, after twenty years of service, with five years active duty in the European and Pacific theaters during World War II.)

How can you respect a man who makes a good speech in Congress about the sanctity of private property and turns right around, at the prompting of his political masterminds, and goes against the very principles he enunciated? And how would you size up the situation when a new Congressman calls for an appointment four days hence with a bureau head, but three days hence his father arrives to request that as a consultant he'd appreciate small businesses being referred to him? And this is the same father who has never owned his own business but who enjoys a sizable ARA grant at Atlanta University to help advise Negroes in starting their own businesses. Why was this report delayed in the Atlanta Newspapers, Inc., a couple months until it could be quietly and unobtrusively slipped in, and why was not this grant given to some deserving Negro Ph.D. or Negro businessman? These are questions that a gentleman cannot ask during a campaign; but as a Christian, and one interested in good government, I ask them now. No matter how many years people may say "Honorable" before his name, he must still look himself in the mirror and face the man he is.

Mary M. O'Callaghan

Jim did not expect to run in this second race, nor did anyone urge him to. Quite the contrary! But when no known Republican would present himself to challenge the suicidal, bankrupting, socialistic trend the national government had adopted, there was no choice but to put up our $750 qualifying fee, roll up our sleeves, and pitch in. While this might have been an opportunity for some people, victory would have been a decided sacrifice for Jim and our family. However, people who are not willing to sacrifice and fight for Christianity are not Christians, and people who are not willing to fight and sacrifice for their country are not patriots. I consider these two things worth fighting for to preserve for my children. I really didn't pitch in as much to be a steadfast wife as I did to be a daughter steadfast to the principles my father and mother always upheld as dear, and to be a steadfast mother, that my children might inherit something better than the Great Society — socialism by another name.

Yes, Joe, the race had to be run and has to continue to be run, for communism has declared war on God. Those of us on God's side, you and I, must be wise and alert to recognize the war within and without our country. When the enemy is invited to sup at our table and spread his propaganda over our own TV, and share our secrets through laxity and corruption in high places, and seduce us to completely disarm ourselves, whom can we blame but ourselves when he does what he says he'll do and buries us? He predicts it will even be our own choice. Well, I don't so choose!

(1998 note — Khrushchev was America's invited guest, and now Gorbachev is headquartered in San Francisco, with his expenses paid by American taxpayers, with freedom to our patent office among his other privileges. I didn't vote for that, and I resent the intrusion into my country and into my bank account! They said we'd vote for it. And they will assure it by illegal methods if legal ones won't work.)

Joe, I know our views differ, and I should not take advantage of your kind letter to blow off steam; but when this all means enough to me to go through what we just went through, I find it hard to bottle it up. Since you respected us enough to write us a letter, I'm honest enough to spout my true feelings.

You made a statement in our church, agreeing with the principle of "taking from the haves to give to the have-nots." Can you honestly think that socialism can ever be a characteristic of the land of opportunity?

Having sought nothing for ourselves in this race, we have lost nothing. And it was no secret that we personally did not want to move to Washington. Thank you

The Government Shall Be Upon Whose Shoulder?

again for your letter. May you and yours have a wonderful and prosperous New Year.

                Mary O'Callaghan
                Atlanta, Georgia

                                              December 6, 1965

Dr. Sanford Atwood, President, Emory University
Atlanta, Georgia

Dear Dr. Atwood,

    Since my most valuable possessions have been entrusted to the care of your institution, I beg a few moments of your valuable time.
    I realize your position in this "atheist" turmoil and I readily admit my own very strong position in upholding our freedoms, praying we may always have freedom of choice. For a Christian, the choice of an educational institution is naturally one of bias. If I were not interested in my child furthering his Christian education I would not choose a church-oriented school. Since I am, and since I did, or thought I did, and am choosing to pay dearly for this, I expect him to come forth from four years under that influence a stronger Christian than when he went in. If we do not choose in the light of our prejudgments, of what use is education or experience?
    I consider myself neither a crackpot nor an extremist, but I am extremely alarmed at what I see happening to my country because Christians will not exercise their freedom of speech. I will apologize to no atheist for my faith. I am a graduate of Randolph-Macon Woman's College, Phi Beta Kappa, which may help you understand the importance I attach to higher education but it is as nothing to me compared with the importance of a strong Christian faith, the basis of all of life. Education alone does not prepare a person to live fully.

Mary M. O'Callaghan

Of my six children, one has already graduated from Emory and one will graduate in June. I do not want my other four children under that same influence, which I feel has failed a sacred trust. Why should I pay to have deliberately undermined the thing I consider most precious in life? The faith I uphold has been undermined, and you are supporting this tragedy in the name of free speech with Professor Althizer's "God is dead" profession. I do not believe he was advertised as an atheist for all parents and students to freely exercise a choice. I don't mind a Buddhist briefly explaining his views, or a Hindu, or one of another religion, but in comparative religion for a concentrated quarter's study, a so-called Christian university is obligated to provide a Christian to expound the Christian faith. These are years of questioning and searching for young adults, as they should be. Give the atheists this time of a young person's life and you are apt to give them his life. I deeply resent what I feel is a fraud perpetrated against me, and yet you uphold him rather than those who have been defrauded. False prophets should be thrown out rather than coddled. Let him wear the atheist label publicly somewhere else, but don't hide him in a Christian role in a Christian school.

Dr. Atwood, I am as concerned for this whole "undedicated" generation as I am for my own children. I pray Christians can look to Christian leadership for help not only in propagating the Gospel but also in keeping our country free.

Sincerely,
Mary M. O'Callaghan

Christmas Newsletter — 1965

The calendar confirms that Christmas is here once again, though our spring-like weather denies it and my graying head shakes that " 'tain't possible"! When years fly by, it's a sign of you-know-what, and when your husband has crossed the half-century mark (and proud to have made it!), you can only conclude that you are getting old; and isn't it fun?!!!

The O'Callaghans have had a wonderful, busy year and the Lord has blessed us with health and happiness, though we manage to zip through the wealth in record time! Wendy, Laurie and I made our annual jaunt to Florida in May with Jim's mother and Aunt "Ceal" from Nashville, laden with schoolbooks, along with golf clubs, shell books, and sand and water equipment. We were thrilled at the Prince of Peace exhibit, where we stole a peek over the fence at the artist working on a new scene in the life of Christ. The figures and backgrounds in the diorama let you participate in those important events in the Holy Land. We encountered (which is the only way to describe it) the deer at the Deer Ranch, and we cruised through the jungle where the Tarzan movies were filmed, all at Silver Springs. We left Tarzan's monkeys swinging through the trees and proceeded via Cypress Gardens and their breathtaking water show to Naples for two weeks.

Karen was one of four first-honor graduates (all 4.0 average) at Northside High, so her daddy rewarded her with a flight down to join us for a few days before graduation. Karen flew to Houston this spring to look over Rice University, but she chose Vanderbilt as her alma mater. She's working hard there, with her fingers in many pies — AOPi pledge, hall president, Student Christian Council, Conservative Club, Young Republicans, etc. — and she calls college life a veritable dream world!

Jimbo is winding up his senior year at Emory, and he has been accepted at Georgia Medical College in Augusta. Our original figure of twenty-four years of college education is lengthening! Cindy chose summer school this summer to allow more time for activities during her junior year. She keeps the Teen Republicans going and busies herself at church and school. She turned sweet sixteen in August, to become the sixth driver in the family.

The big event of the year was Marky's wedding on August 7. She wanted a small wedding, but she had promised so many little cousins over the years, "Sure,

Mary M. O'Callaghan

you can be in my wedding," that she had to have a big one. Her cousin Pat "O'C" was maid of honor; a neighbor and two former roommates, along with Karen and Cindy, were bridesmaids; and junior bridesmaids included Wendy and Laurie and three little cousins. As they came down the aisle you could hear the whispers, "That's a sister. That's a cousin. That's a sister," etc., etc. In spite of the horrendous downpour at the worst time, people have told me they never saw a happier wedding. She married George MacNabb, a senior medical student at Emory from Newnan, Georgia, and we heartily approve of our new son and all his family. They have an apartment not too far from us. Marky still teaches high school, as well as going to night school to get her hours for certification.

Jim continues to enjoy managing the Mutual Funds Department for Courts & Company, which has entailed a little traveling. I slipped aboard in August to combine a little pleasure with business. The men hit Philadelphia and Wall Street and we shuttled to Boston, all in one day. After business, we were free to drink in early American atmosphere in New England and stand in awe where Pilgrims had stood, swelling with pride at our heritage. We toured Cape Cod, along with hundreds of others, and liked best our stay on Nantucket Island, bicycling among artists' studios and whaling relics and eating that scrumptious swordfish. Martha's Vineyard was fun, too, before a day at the World's Fair and then home to rest.

Our new golf club has just opened, the Atlanta Country Club, so maybe I can cope with it better than with the goat hills at Cherokee. Jim manages to "check the real estate" several times a week, and I'm hoping to do a little more ball watching myself on our new course.

As the sun sinks slowly in the golden west and as the year slips into oblivion, all the O'Callaghans wish all of you a happy and blessed Christmas and a wonderful year to come!

Commentary — 1965

These were days of verbal combat, a cold war waged for the minds (the souls) of men. Truly, the mind is the battlefield where Satan's messengers (the Greek word is the same word as the one for "angels") plant ideas to exalt man above God. Satan parades as an angel of light, with enticing counterfeits to draw men from God. The attractive lure ends in destruction, and the promises of the "now" overshadow the consequences of the future. Even the very elect may be deceived! Jesus explained all parables by the parable of the sower (Mark 4:13 ff). The sower sows the word. Jesus said His words were spirit and they were life (John 6:63). Jesus speaks of Satan as the thief who comes to steal and kill and destroy (John 10:10). Since everything produces after its own kind (Genesis 1) and seedtime and harvest will not cease as long as the Earth remains (Genesis 8:22), Satan tries to pervert God's seeds and produce his own harvest of death and destruction instead of a harvest of life. Death and life are in the power of the tongue (Proverbs 18:21). Words are seeds, producing harvests.

One such word perverted to brainwash the people is the word PEACE. Watching the country being brainwashed by manipulators, instead of being washed by the water of the Word (Ephesians 5:26), Mary included an addendum letter to her Christmas message to those who were politically minded.

"Peace", the Christmas cards proclaim this year as never before, but let no Christian mistake the peace of God for the peace of surrender. War has been declared against God, and Christians are compelled to arm for the combat. Atheists and Communists make full use of the freedom of speech while Christians, by their silence, condemn civilization, as we know it. "Freedom" has been translated into licentiousness, illicit love, pornography and violence, but the U.S. Supreme Court denies children the freedom to say, "Thank you, God" in school, and even privately over their lunch. Christians must uphold constituted law and change laws where needed; but strangely enough, it was forty-three local Christian clergy and educators and the National Council of Churches falsely claiming to testify "in the name of forty million Christians," who dealt the most damaging blows to the Becker Amendment. That amendment sought to give us the

Mary M. O'Callaghan

right to VOTE whether or not we wanted Bible reading and prayers in our particular public schools. Now that we have safely protected innocent children from God, Christians will be happy to know that once they have erred from God's ways, our courts WILL allow Bible reading and prayers in public prisons.

We live in a "Great Society" that magnanimously dispenses all God's material gifts in the name of government and a loving President. So who needs God? Christians have remained silent too long over racial injustices; and now they remain silent when, in the name of antipoverty, our federal funds support such projects as the Black Arts Repertory Theater-School in Harlem ($40,000 publicly acknowledged) where hatred of white people, and violence, are taught proudly. Though times are admittedly prosperous, our national leaders are willingly and wittingly leading our nation into deeper indebtedness and bankruptcy because the bought vote is the sure vote and lust for power blinds to the sacred trust of the nation.

Every Christian American must hang his head at the dastardly surrender of free peoples as secretly perpetrated by our elected President at Yalta, Teheran and Potsdam, and our surrender of China, which gave away almost half the world to communists. In spite of this, and though this one White House family represents eight divorces now, the Roman Catholic authority here declared special dispensation to eat meat on Friday so that Catholics would attend a Democratic fund-raising dinner to hear F. D. Roosevelt, Jr.

In *Reflections On The Failure of Socialism*, which should be required reading for all believers in the Great Society, Max Eastman points out that the greatest enemy of human hope is not the brute facts, evident for all to see, but the intelligentsia who will not face them. Or as Christians interpret it, they have eyes to see but will not see, and ears to hear but will not hear.

I pray God's peace for our boys in Vietnam. Our nation responded to the desperate call of a nation facing the onslaught of communism. However, we prevented our offensive forces from moving beyond a certain parallel and for the first time in our history did not win in combat because the powers that be did not want a victory! Why sacrifice in a war you don't intend to win?

Though our conscience is smitten by our treachery to freedom-loving Cubans, I pray for wisdom and caution in allowing Cubans unquestioned access to our country. Cuba has been a dedicated training ground for Communist infiltration, sabotage, and violence in our hemisphere. Will we lend a hand to our own destruc-

The Government Shall Be Upon Whose Shoulder?

tion after cold-bloodedly dealing a deathblow to Cuban freedom hopes? There will be no honorable peace in this world until we have righted the wrongs committed against these fellowmen whom we have subjected to Communist slavery. Shall we settle for dishonorable peace?

Christmas is for Christians, to keep and proclaim. It is a message of peace and love and hope — but not worldly peace, nor love of safety and power, nor hope for worldly goods in a Great Society.

Christmas is a message nailed to a cross.

Author's Note

While Christians were uneasy about the proclamations of the National Council of Churches of Christ in America, which claimed to speak for forty million Christians in America, there seemed to be little they could do about it but murmur and complain! The NCCCA was so constituted that denominations, not individual congregations, joined as members, and the denominations were assessed per capita count of their total denomination. An individual or a church could be extremely disenchanted by the left-wing pronouncements, projects and scope of the NCCCA, but with no recourse. They could adamantly protest and withhold their financial support but the denomination paid, nevertheless, simply taking from Peter to pay for Paul! There were always enough charitable projects to fool the unsuspecting and naive Christian leaders to add validity to and disguise the underlying purposes of the organization. The NCCCA has followed the Communist party goals and still does in 1998, aiming towards a one-world religion under a one-world government as constituted by the United Nations. National sovereignty must go!

The following letter is included as one response to the 1965 Christmas messages. A friend shared them with her brother and sister-in-law, whose names have been changed to protect privacy.

February 6, 1966

Dear Mary,

Betty and George shared with us the letter you enclosed in your Christmas card, and it made a very deep impression on Bill and me. We have been concerned about our nation getting so far away from God and the principles that this country was founded upon and for the apathy of the American people in letting so many things come to pass to which we object and which we know are wrong.

We number ourselves among them, as our actions have been only to vote and "shoot off our mouths." After your letter, we went to our precinct meeting and are delegates to the County and State Conventions. We may not become active in politics, but we will have a better understanding and speak with a little more

The Government Shall Be Upon Whose Shoulder?

authority and take a more active part in combating some of the mistakes that have been made. I thought you might like to know the effect you had.

Your letter was in the same vein that our church has been preaching for several months. I am going to read it to our circle this week, and our minister has asked for a copy to use. We would like your permission to make copies of it to pass among our Christian friends, and I would like to send it to our national church magazine, *The Lutheran Witness*. I don't know that they will publish it, but I hope so. Would you mind?

       Cordially,
       Sally and Bill Smith

Update — 1998

The denominations that still belong to the National Council of Churches have found their membership rolls perceptibly dwindling. The years have proven NCCCA's unchanging allegiance to stated Communist objectives.

I was nine years old when the Great Depression struck. Franklin Roosevelt started entitlements to begin a social welfare system for the first time in American history. His New Deal set the stage for government to dominate American business, banks, commerce and our economy. In the sixties Lyndon Johnson increased the welfare funding, declaring a "war on poverty" in his "Great Society." The system was built on borrowing without the ability to pay, but it guaranteed votes! Our government incurred debts, which required payment of interest, which required more borrowing, while the debt kept growing. Government and spending have burgeoned together. The cure built on national debt has proven worse than the problem, with our national deficit now in the trillions and growing! Communism has bred socialism, which has bred liberalism, which is breeding a New World Order, or to be currently "politically correct," a Global Village!

HAVE YOU CHECKED THE TEMPERATURE OF THE WATER LATELY?

Christmas Greetings — 1966

The long-awaited day is nigh — the climax of the year and of life itself, when we celebrate the arrival of God on Earth! As we rummage in the attic among old familiar boxes for those beloved glittering symbols of seasonal joy, our memories come tumbling out also. We dust off and cherish the patina that years have added to these precious reminiscences, and are exceedingly thankful for those loved ones who made them possible. We realize that happy memories are among the most precious gifts we can give to our children and that that is what life is all about — loving and being loved — and that that is why God gave us Christmas! It is the loveliest of gifts and surpasses all glory and human imaginings, and to the year's trials and tribulations, sacrifices and pleasures it adds a divine depth of meaning. Emmanuel! God with us!

Among these precious memories are friendships and kinships worth more than pure gold. As each card is addressed and sent to someone special, our love and thoughts and best wishes go "special delivery" too!

The years continue to bless the O'Callaghan family with good health and much happiness, wherein lies our wealth! Son-in-law George graduated from Emory Medical School in June and happily got an internship in internal medicine at Grady Hospital here, so Marky has continued to teach at O'Keefe High. The "Dr. MacNabbs" still have an apartment around the corner from my mother. Navy duty stares him in the face, either offshore or in Vietnam. It breaks my heart that this generation has to suffer the same separations and war trials that we did! Son Jim graduated from Emory and is now studying at Georgia Medical College in Augusta.

Karen's Daddy joined the Phoenix Society and at a lovely Thanksgiving ball he, along with thirty other beaming fathers, proudly presented his daughter to society. This was preceded by an informal presentation of the group in June, and many gala and "fantabulous" assorted parties during the summer, with more to come this Christmas. Karen worked with the other Phoenix debutantes at the Easter Seal Rehabilitation Center and ate the whole procedure up with a spoon! She's on the Dean's List at Vanderbilt.

Cindy and I have been touring college campuses, and if the miracle doesn't come through to admit her to William and Mary (they take only thirty percent out-

Mary M. O'Callaghan

of-state students), she'll probably go to Vanderbilt or Emory in September. She was awarded the Service Cup for her class last year and is now working hard as Editor of her Annual, among other school, church, and political activities. She spent eight weeks this summer at Hidden Valley Camp near Chattanooga in the Counselor-in-training program. Wendy and Laurie joined her there for their first four-week stay away from home — a marvelous experience for all! While they were gone, my sister Dot Kendrick with her daughter, Mary Ann, drove to Atlanta from Texas to show off her son Bill's precious two year old blonde daughter.

Jim and I made trips separately and together to Florida, and then Highlands, North Carolina; and his mother and Aunt "Ceal," Wendy, Laurie and I made our annual two-week jaunt to Naples, Florida, in May. Some year the school is going to say something about my taking them out, but we do carry books and assignments and have a VERY educational time!

When Jim and I attended a Mutual Funds Conference in Washington the last of October, these too-lengthy Christmas epistles almost came to an end! Take my advice and don't get on a four-engine plane that loses two engines on one side on takeoff and has landing gear trouble, to boot. We soared over Washington at about two hundred fifty feet, and twenty-five minutes and many prayers later we landed south of there (our destination was north) at Andrews Air Force Base, midst fire engines, ambulances and a helicopter to spray us if necessary. Though we landed without mishap, it was an experience we wouldn't care to repeat. All our pilot friends tell us you simply don't walk away from that set of circumstances. On landing we all took a deep breath, thanking the Lord, I'm sure, and applauded! They didn't even give us so much as a Coca-Cola when they sent the very same kind of plane to take us on to New York. My brother Curtis and Colette joined us there for dinner and a hilarious Sam Levene show. The next morning we flew to Bermuda for a few days of sight-seeing, motor biking, swimming at the pink beaches, and soaking up the British accent.

If you have been reading financial magazines you know that Jim, as manager of the Mutual Funds Department of Courts & Company, has helped put together a mutual funds retirement program for TVA. I understand an interview is in the December 19 *Newsweek*. I hope they are not as agile at misquoting as our Atlanta press. He loves his work downtown, but still goes out to his "country office" several times a week (for eighteen or nineteen holes).

My golf endeavors have been mostly confined to out-of-town trips, which is

The Government Shall Be Upon Whose Shoulder?

no way to accomplish lower than a max handicap. Some year I guess I'll just have to quit teaching Sunday school, working in our church baby clinic, taking Wendy and Laurie to band practice, and leading their Scout troop, and take up golf seriously!

We worked real hard to get Bo Callaway elected Governor and Fletcher Thompson Congressman. Fletcher made it, but it surely is hard to get a Republican Governor when the Democrats have made all the rules for generations. We haven't given up yet, despite the Supreme Court, and are thrilled at the gains across the nation.

Memories go on and on, but we'll close and wish YOU and YOURS a memorable Christmas and New Year ahead.

Mary and Jim
Marky, Jimbo, Karen, Cindy, Wendy and Laurie

Commentary — 1966

In 1966 the Republicans were still battling for an effective and vibrant two-party system in Georgia. When persistent and valiant efforts were finally rewarded by a Republican Fifth District Congressman, the O'Callaghans were honestly glad it was not Jim's year for candidacy. The caustic tongue of the liberal press grinds into mincemeat the flesh, bones, hair, teeth, breath and very shadow of a conservative!

Commentary — 1967

The leaven of Communist goals in America has been diligently and methodically sprinkled and stirred into all strata and ages of our society. Activated by un-American forensic, it has bubbled up visibly in violent outbreaks. Race, war, poverty, coexistence — every human need and aspiration and frustration has been accentuated and activated to breed distrust, discontent and demonstration. College campuses, in a nation upholding freedom of speech, have been and are being targeted to capture the minds of the intellectual youths.

I quote from a letter written in February 1967, from daughter Karen, a sophomore at Vanderbilt University, Nashville, Tennessee:

"Everyone wants one thing, to be happy. God gave us this desire to find happiness, and through Christ, the way to find happiness. But He also gave us certain mental and emotional makeups, certain talents, which, added to environmental influences, make us need to express ourselves and find complete fulfillment in different ways. I have to be wise to be happy; I have to know and understand people; I have to think and learn and know the truth. If you are ever going to do anyone any good you must be wise, and to be wise you have to have experiences."

Karen was in the throes of life-determining decisions, such as career choice, and the optimum opportunity toward that goal. She realized the limitations of her chosen political science major and the complications that a future family (also a part of fulfillment) would add to an active political career. She wanted to "take my future into my hands rather than drift into it." She wanted to reach beyond her comfortable Southern background and touch the reality of the world. She was "content" with her college, but found "zero intellectual atmosphere, and little, precious little, stimulation in the classroom politically. What good is a seventy-five percent conservative school when nobody does anything, and most people could care less." (I might add, what good is the Body of Christ that has been called forth to subdue the Earth and take dominion over it, when all it wants to do is examine its own warts and not soil its hands with government?)

To further quote Karen, "The other day I was talking with two graduate students from Turkey. One of them was leaving Saturday to go back and start a

The Government Shall Be Upon Whose Shoulder?

Communist revolution. I talked for two hours and a half with these boys. Have you *ever* talked to a Communist about politics, religion or anything even? It's a frightening experience, but it was even more, a broadening one." On page ten she closed: "Good night and God bless. I remember you all each night in my prayers, and I hope you do me also. Love, Karen." And after a P.S. she added a long P.P.S., concerning my views about a certain school to which she was considering transferring: "It half made me mad and has really bothered me that you said you don't want me 'up there with all those Communists and beatniks and stuff.' I don't understand at all. Don't you think that I'm smart enough to have thought out carefully what I believe, and examined it well enough to know it's true? Even since talking with those two boys I have a lot of respect for some Communists. But they are wrong as they can be. Do you think that I believe what I do just because of yours and Daddy's political views? If I do, then you are right. I might be just as molded by someone who has a strong influence on me and who is a leftist. But before anyone could change my political views, they would have to change my whole view on life and way of thinking. Maybe they could, but I seriously doubt it."

Karen was expressing the maturity of her own views and strengths, without really rebelling from parental guidance. This urge for self-realization burns in the bosom of all idealistic youth, to see a better future and create a world better than the one their eyes behold. Where we the Church have done a proper job, this idealism is founded on Jesus and imposes spiritual values to correct wrongs. Where the Church has failed, this same idealism becomes an explosive bomb of unrealistic utopia, fused by perverted promises, rebellion from responsibilities, commitment to false concepts, and death and destruction. They admit that the way to that utopia requires, first of all, total extinction of all opposition. Then peace will reign supreme. That is a perversion of the responsible choice offered by the Prince of Peace.

The rebellion of these times — reflected in long unkempt hair, hippie and yippee cultures, communes, drug scenes, demonstrations and riots, adultery, divorce — stems from the perversion of God's call to know Him and have dominion over the Earth. Ultimate peace can come only through Jesus, the Prince of Peace.

Christmas Newsletter — 1967

Once again we join in the joyous celebration of the coming of the Christ, Emmanuel, God with us! The love we share with Him, our family and friends ripens into golden fruit as the years speed pell-mell by. The O'Callaghans can truly be thankful for a cup running over with the good things of life — health, happiness, and beloved friends, as well as bounties of the earth to share. We pray your blessings include these fruits also!

My New Year's resolution to take things easier was foiled before the year began, when I agreed to chair the women's board of our church baby clinic. For forty-five years Central Presbyterian Church has operated a free sick baby clinic for those who don't qualify for other facilities. Just to complicate my job, we've had to call a new minister who will come this month, we have secured a new medical director as of this month, and we have moved into our new building which is still not completely equipped. We do have wonderful doctors who volunteer their time, some for many years, including Jewish doctors. I did quit teaching Sunday school in June.

My Junior Girl Scout troop wound up the school year with a two-night campout, and then I moved up with Wendy into Cadette Scouting. I now have twenty-seven seventh-, eighth-, and ninth-grade girls bouncing around our house every Tuesday night. We had a weekend campout in late September simultaneously with a record cold wave. There's no better way to get acquainted than to huddle around a campfire. We are now frantically making and selling Christmas items to finance a charter bus trip to Williamsburg, Virginia, in mid-January. Would you believe we need eight hundred dollars? There's a method in my madness, because Cindy is enjoying her freshman year at William and Mary and I'll have an extra chance to see her. She graduated first in her class, with several others who made all A's. She tried out for it and gave the valedictory address.

This year we waited until June for our Florida trip and took a house for six weeks at Siesta Key, Sarasota. There was much coming and going — Cindy, Wendy, Laurie and Chopper stayed the whole time; Jim commuted several times; both grandmothers and a cousin visited, as well as a couple sets of guests for Cindy; Karen took time off from her job at Rich's to visit; Jimbo took a week off

The Government Shall Be Upon Whose Shoulder?

from the Pathology Department at St. Joseph's Hospital to drive down with a friend; Marky and George spent a couple days on their way to Key West, Florida, where George reported for Navy duty after his year of internship at Grady Hospital; Carolyn and Richard O'Callaghan and their two youngest girls joined us briefly and held down the fort while I flew home for a Courts & Company dinner announcing the new partners, of which Jim is one. After studying the courses and taking a stiff Stock Exchange exam, the new partnerships became effective November 1.

In the spring, Jim and I did manage to combine a bit of golf with business at Ponte Vedra, Florida, and Southern Pines, North Carolina, and I drove to Clinton, South Carolina, with Jim for a board meeting of Presbyterian College.

We did win one political campaign in the family — Wendy was elected Co-Captain of the School Patrol, which means she has to get there early. "Now you tell me!" she said, a true O'Callaghan. Despite Laurie's laziness with the saxophone all summer, she managed to make the Northside Highlander Elementary Band, part of a terrific city band program. They hope to go to Pittsburgh this spring.

Karen and her Vanderbilt roommate transferred to the University of Wisconsin in Madison, to broaden their educational base. She characterized the students as men and women, not college kids — all studying hard and planning on graduate school. But her last letter had them pegged as psychos and neurotics, with speaker systems announcing such-and-such demonstrations at such-and-such places! She and Christy are running as conservatives in the Young Republican group, so I'm anxious to know the outcome. She takes skiing and is saving her pennies to go to Europe when she graduates. She wants to put into practice all the German, French and Spanish she has taken. She'll probably learn some Italian before she goes!

The summer was climaxed with a wonderful Mees family reunion. Sister Dot Kendrick drove here with daughter Mary Ann from Abilene, Texas, by way of New Orleans to pick up granddaughter Kim. Grandpa Dick joined them later. Brother Curtis and Colette Mees drove down from New Jersey with their two daughters. With Don's crew of five we all spent the day at Six Flags Over Georgia. There's nothing like a great family celebration!

For those who do not have a fun and wonderful family with whom to celebrate, may I remind you that Jesus came to let us know about our wonderful

Mary M. O'Callaghan

Heavenly Father. There's a great big worldwide family out there to get acquainted with and enjoy. A church family is very special, and they need exactly what you may have to offer. Try it; you'll like it! And Jesus will too!

Christmas Newsletter — 1968

With coattails flying, the O'Callaghans are hanging onto the caboose of 1968 as it speeds across the horizon. With one hand free we'll wave you a cheery MERRY CHRISTMAS and HAPPY NEW YEAR before it rushes out of sight!

Old '68 got off to a quick start and the pace only accelerated. In January my Cadette Girl Scout troop climaxed weeks of preparation with a bus trip to Williamsburg, Yorktown and Jamestown, Virginia. Cindy was happily able to leave exams at William and Mary long enough to join us.

Shortly thereafter, business called Jim to New York. We decided to take Wendy and Laurie (twelve and ten), and even talked Jim's mother into her first flight! It was such fun making her lifetime dream come true as we whisked her from museums to Wall Street, from Chinatown's riotous New Year's fireworks to Greenwich Village, from the Statue of Liberty to the United Nations Building, and even, by accident, by subway, to the snow-covered aquarium at Coney Island! It was also another good occasion to see my brother Curtis and Colette and their two girls from New Jersey.

Jim had a Palm Springs convention in February, and Wendy, Laurie and I were included at the very last minute. He couldn't stand to be that close to Disneyland without taking them. As we made a turn over the Pacific Ocean on our return flight from Los Angeles; they didn't think it differed much from the Atlantic Ocean.

I weathered a couple spring campouts with my scouts, and Laurie went with her band to Pittsburgh. Such remarks were heard: "They couldn't possibly be grammar school children; they must be midgets." Laurie blows a mean saxophone!

On May 12, Jim's mother summoned us to her apartment about 1:00 AM, not feeling well. It was indeed a sad Mother's Day for us to have to call the rest of the family from the hospital by early morning that she had passed away quite suddenly. Family came from Nashville, and Marky, though pregnant, boarded the train from Key West. We drove her back, adding a few days of rest in Florida.

In June we hosted a dinner-dance with other Phoenix Society members for Cindy and their daughters. She partied on many fun occasions until midsummer, before reporting to North Carolina to counsel at camp.

Mary M. O'Callaghan

Taking the plunge, we bought a "cooperative" apartment in Naples, Florida, which happily necessitated several trips for furnishings. After a couple of trips to Asheville to see Cindy, in August Mother, Wendy and I drove to Abilene, Texas, for Mary Ann Kendrick's wedding. We enjoyed sights and family, and on our return trip Mother even frolicked with us at Six Flags Over Texas.

What a great day September 27 was when Mary Lisa MacNabb arrived, in Key West. "Grandma O'C" headed to Florida immediately to help bathe, bottle and burp. Grandpa was not too far behind.

The Phoenix Thanksgiving ball was a gala occasion. Karen spent Thanksgiving with her roommate in Chicago. They worked all summer to save up money for a European jaunt when they graduate from the University of Wisconsin. She's been active in politics (Republican, of course) and will tour again with the University Singers. I hope to get up there to see if they are as good as she claims, and the campus as beautiful.

Jim continues to love his work and golfs regularly. As with most years, we tasted some of the bitter as well as the sweet of life. We are ever grateful for our wonderful family, friends and faith that give meaning to it all. God rest you merry, Gentle Friends.

P.S. To Republicans only — Wasn't that a great way to wind up the year?!!!

Commentary — 1968

Despite the dire predictions of the Democrats after the 1964 Goldwater defeat that the Republican Party was dead and could be laid to rest, Richard Nixon was elected President, along with many Republican Governors. Johnson's "Great Society," with its numerous unsuccessful social welfare programs, was laid to rest instead.

Update — 1998

Looking back over the intervening thirty years, one must wonder what difference it makes who is elected, because the power that runs the nation is behind the scenes, naming and bankrolling candidates in both parties. Those who propose other than the "politically correct global party line" to complete the forty-five objectives previously listed, plus more, and so eliminate national sovereignties will find their character assassinated and their political careers in the obituary columns. Power-mad internationalists are calling the shots. That appears to be very literal, as "suicides," "accidents," unexplained "plane crashes," etc., have left a trail of the bodies of any who might effectively expose the truth.

The amazing thing is that the Bible has already exposed the truth, in both the Tanakh (Old Testament) and the New Testament! Not only has it exposed the final worldwide dictatorship, but it lets all those involved know that they will spend eternity in a lake of fire where there will be perpetual weeping and wailing and gnashing of teeth. God doesn't want anyone to thus perish, so Jesus came to forgive all repentant sinners and make a place for them in Glory. That is the message for which Christians all over the world are risking torture, life and limb to tell those who may not have heard. But Pharaoh's heart was hardened! Where there is no repentance, God hardens the heart more.

THERE IS SOMEONE IN THE BOILING POT WITH CHRISTIANS, INSULATING US!

Hallelujah! Christmas Newsletter — 1969

As rapidly fleeting years antique our lives, the patina of friendships glows more golden and precious. But how pointless would be the memories of the years, the activities of the days, and the dreams of the future without that Divine Gift bestowed on mankind in the fullness of time! One of the happiest parts of celebrating that greatest of gifts is the polishing up of old and valued friendships, sending our warmest wishes for health and happiness!

For the O'Callaghans, 1969 has been a mixture of trials and triumphs. "Rafferty Reagan" joined the household last Christmas morning, all his toy poodle apricot glory tucked in a surprise stocking for Mom. He has helped fill the void left by the disappearance of "Chopper," but his penchant for chewing up tooth retainers, sax mouthpieces, etc., has left a void in Dad's wallet.

Wendy, Laurie and Mom flew to Wisconsin for a firsthand glimpse of the University and a performance of the University Singers, which has been such a fun thing for Karen. After her graduation, Karen flew to Taiwan with the Youth Crusade for Freedom, as a guest of the Republic of China, for a five-week travel and study visit. (How many parents have daughters who can spout Chinese expletives when the occasion arises?) They can be added to a very short list of civilian personnel who have been allowed to go to Quemoy in recent years, flying the last twenty-five miles about fifty feet over the water. She was delighted with the thrills of a new country and new friendships, and we were delighted with her safe return. She lingered in California long enough to locate a theatrical agent, and came home long enough to earn money to get back out there. She is now at the Hollywood Studio Club run by the YWCA, planning to enter drama school; so if anyone knows any friends for the friendless (almost) out that way, please speak up!

Cindy spent her summer directing horseback at Camp MerriMac in Black Mountain, North Carolina. Since her field is really water-front safety instruction, she literally and figuratively struggled to stay one jump ahead of the girls. She had such a blast she wants to do it again next summer. She mixes Kappa Kappa Gamma activities with water ballet, choir, chorus and an interesting curriculum this junior year at William and Mary. (We have our own Pan-Hellenic Council, with Mom Phi Mu, Marky Tri-Delta, Karen AOPi, Dad SPE and Jimbo KA, and still two girls to go!)

The Government Shall Be Upon Whose Shoulder?

Jimbo continues to be deeply involved in his senior year of medicine at Augusta. Being in the Navy program, he has applied for a Navy internship. Son-in-law George MacNabb will complete his three-year Navy tour in June when he, Marky and Lisa will bid farewell to Key West and settle back here for several more years of residency at Grady Hospital. They were fortunate to have spent the whole tour of duty in Key West. Two doting grandparents can hardly wait to start the spoiling process.

Several visits to Naples have confirmed our evaluation that our little apartment is truly a corner of paradise. It was a fun and hectic paradise this summer with ten people and three dogs, and only two bedrooms and two baths, one weekend. Our neighbors are delightful, shelling is fun, fishing is good even from our back wall, we've been introduced to sailing, and we've about learned to dock the boat without knocking over the dock!

With everyone else scattered, it is a joy to have Wendy (ninth grade) and Laurie (seventh) at home to keep the hearthside merry. Wendy is presently enjoying a modeling course. Laurie was among some in her band to make the All-State Band. A ski trip to Beech Mountain, North Carolina, several campouts, advanced camping and sailing training courses for Mom, and a craft fair to earn money for a week's trip to Florida next summer have all crowded the Scout agenda.

The most changes have been in the business world. It was a great loss early in the year when "Wag" Wagner, who ran one of the O'Callaghan companies, died quite suddenly. Mother worked there four days a week and finally retired, well after her eightieth birthday. She remains in right good health and lives in Atlanta with her sister, not far from us. Younger brother Richard O'Callaghan, who runs the other company, Dealers Supply, suffered a second heart attack this fall but is recuperating well. The real shocker came when Courts & Company, unbeknownst to most of the partners, including Jim on the Executive Committee, was given away to Reynolds & Company. The entire industry is almost as shocked as those people who had devoted their lives for years to a company so casually and suddenly given away out from under them. Jim has not reached a decision about a permanent move, but is listening with interest to all prospects.

The Light that shone in the darkness long ago still shines to change sorrow into peace, desolation into hope, hatred into compassion, and bondage into freedom. We rejoice with you at the divine miracle of Emmanuel, God With Us!

Commentary — 1969

Riots and bloodshed continued on college campuses. In disturbances the University of Wisconsin probably ranked second after Berkeley. Mary took Wendy and Laurie to Madison, before Karen's graduation. Looking in on the melee in the student union, Karen remarked that there was probably more brainpower gathered together in that place than anywhere in the country. One glance evoked the response from Mary, "Yes, and they are all sick."

Karen was one of three students interviewed and pictured in *U.S. News & World Report* as a conservative on that liberal campus. With tongue in cheek on St. Patrick's Day the conservatives submitted to the State Legislature their demands for Green Power, from Karen O'Callaghan and her Irish minority at the university. They demanded shamrocks to be planted on campus, Gaelic be taught, a department of Irish studies, green beer, a percentage of teachers with "O' " in their names, St. Patrick's Day holiday, etc. The Assembly Journal of the State of Wisconsin, Seventy-ninth Regular Session, Tuesday, March 18, 1969, closed with the words:

"Assemblyman McEssy asked unanimous consent that the assembly adjourn in recognition of, and sympathy to, Karen O'Callaghan (Leader of ISA — Irish Students' Association) in her campaign for Green Power and Irish equality on the University of Wisconsin campus. Granted."

Unpublished Letter to the Editor

Atlanta, Georgia
January 17, 1970

The Editor
Atlanta Journal
Atlanta, Georgia

Dear Sir,

How long will the American people honor the farcical fantasy that a certain racial balance, at a certain time, in a certain place (all variables) magically equals better education or even better race relations? If the intelligent populace, teachers and students, leave the system rather than be forced to submit to a situation deleterious to the educational process, then the net loser is the public school system and the children caught in it.

My husband and I are graduates of the Atlanta and Fulton County school systems; four of our six children are honor graduates and the other two are undergraduates, and one daughter has taught at O'Keefe. We do not intend to see our youngest two children denied the right to a school in the neighborhood in which we chose to establish our home. At the same time, I will not deny someone else's right to the school of his choice. This free choice plan is now under attack as unconstitutional by the social planners who would force us, like belligerent children, to swallow THEIR choice for us. Those who decry racism the loudest are the very ones demanding "solutions" on a completely racial basis!

Because a minister and director of New Hope declares, "We believe that such a system is essential to teach our children to live in today's society and that it will improve the true quality of education," we are expected to swallow this opinion as if it has a basis in fact, which it doesn't. (Sorry, Ed, I love you, but the American system of freedom of choice is too great a price to pay for your controlled society. Does it gall you that the school that your children and mine attend has been unable to attract more than one Negro teacher last year, and no Negro children? Do you feel unloved?)

Mary M. O'Callaghan

I have faith that the American people will not surrender their decision-making rights to ANY group of social planners who would like to usurp them, no matter how high-soundingly they glorify their purposes nor how inevitably they try to brainwash us into believing their conclusions. It is inevitable only to the extent we are willing to let it be. The "today's society" I am preparing my children for is the society where every man stands in his own right as a child of God, NOT where he is pushed or shoved under some collective formula according to the color of his skin. Mister Minister, I do not think this is either unchristian or unconstitutional. Must all the efforts of our public educational system, to determine, develop and supply individual needs, die on the sacrificial altar of "racial balance," whatever that is?

During my husband's four years of service on the Atlanta Board of Education (President at the critical time of integration), they purposed to reduce and eliminate as soon as possible admitted inequities, and to secure the finest educator in the country as our new Superintendent. Accepting the difficult challenge, Dr. John Letson has justified the faith put in him. In order to determine progress, our system must be judged by what it was ten years ago, not by perfection. That is true of churches, ethnic groups and nations, as well.

America has been built on the rights of the individual, and the freedom she proclaimed has been a beacon of hope to downtrodden peoples the world over, for almost two hundred years. The little man has achieved prosperity unsurpassed in any other civilization in all history. Why? Because the government has been limited to only protect the rights of others and the common good. This system has produced more Negro millionaires in America than in any other country at any time in history. I don't demand or expect equality with that, nor do I resent these accomplishments. At no time in history — I repeat NEVER — has an oppressed people been given political power. Here in America, Negroes have attained every elective office so far but the Presidency and Vice Presidency, which is no doubt more than women have accomplished. As a woman, am I oppressed? Am I downtrodden? Ridiculous!

Here's a wrinkle just as ridiculous as a racial balance ratio. According to the January 16 Atlanta Constitution, Judge Frank Hooper expressed concern three times, over the transfer of coaches in the Atlanta system, indicating an amendment PROTECTING them from reassignment by chance might be a part of his final order. (Emphasis mine.) Silent majority, can't we find a judge interested in "protecting" (to use his word) the children, and the teachers also?

The Government Shall Be Upon Whose Shoulder?

Can an educated, scientific nation really fall hook, line and sinker for the Big Lie that integration equals education? Can the Judeo-Christian faith accept the Big Lie that justice equals equality, without condemning our God for not creating us equal? Perhaps that condemnation is one of the real purposes behind the social planners who would dish up to us Utopia their style?

Can freedom of choice really be un-American? Freedom IS choice! Let us remember that where all men are free, they are not equal; where all men are equal, they are not free.

Mary M. (Mrs. L.J.) O'Callaghan

Update — 1998

It is true there have been racial inequities, to our shame, particularly in the South. Our African-Americans have had to struggle to make a place for themselves in a culture that has limited them as to education and economic opportunities. I thank God our culture has changed, and is changing, to give them opportunity to fulfill their destinies. The plight of our Native American Indians is equally shameful, and I pray that is changing, also.

From the time Jim's Atlanta Board of Education was sworn into office (hand on the Bible, "so help me God") they were in the hands of the courts, to implement integration. They managed to effect the change without incident by starting integration with the higher grades first and allowing no outsiders on the campuses. Each year a few more grades were integrated, according to court order, until all was accomplished. Then the social planners decided not enough had chosen to move so they would have to be forced into it! They know best!

The forthcoming global dictatorship will eliminate all freedoms, except for the "elite." The Prince of Peace alone can bring peace and justice!

Christmas Newsletter — 1970

Once again the fragrant cedars and cinnamon aromas, glowing candles, frosty etchings and nippy winds, happy greetings and tender memories all mingle to bombard our senses with the miraculous proclamation of Emmanuel — God with us! An unpretentious birth, yet hailed by stars in the heavens, by wise men from afar, by lowly shepherds in the fields, by proclaiming angels on high, by powerful enemies plotting death, and by you and by us! Center of all history, this babe brings His invitation to all, with an urgent RSVP not to be ignored: Accept? Or reject? God's loving gift to mankind!

This has been a year of decisions and change for the O'Callaghans. When Blair & Company, which Jim was managing in Atlanta, merged, he and Brian Skone teamed up at Paine, Webber, Jackson & Curtis. At last the market is looking up and they have some great things to offer, so Jim is giving it a whirl, though his greatest strength has always been in management. He still "manages" to chase the little white ball through the woods regularly.

In January we decided to dig up lifelong roots and make First Presbyterian Church our new home. We miss seeing our old friends but have made many new ones. I've swapped choir and baby clinic activities for a community training course, "community" being Atlanta's hippie district teeming with young people, all with problems. Time will tell if or what my role will be there. I still have a Cadette Scout troop, and in June thirty of us took a charter bus tour of Florida for eight days. We covered the Stephen Foster Memorial, St. Augustine, The Space Center, Seaquarium at Key Biscayne (missed the President!), Key West (Marky and George entertained us and I got to squeeze Lisa for a couple of days), Naples, an Indian village with alligator wrestling, Busch Gardens in Tampa, Silver Springs and home — exhausted but happy!

We finally graduated from grammar school when Laurie went up to the eighth grade in high school. Schools are a mess here, with dope, pills, pornography, etc., problems. Our Shangri-La in Naples is a lure, but we can't get away and enjoy it much.

Wendy has taken up jazz this fall and has counted the minutes to December 14, when she can get her learner's driving permit. Cindy is busy this senior year at William and Mary as President of Mortarboard, a Mermettes precision swimmer

Mary M. O'Callaghan

again, a flute player in the orchestra, etc. We were mighty proud that she was chosen for Who's Who in Colleges. She's made a couple of trips to Fort Knox to see Bill MacNabb, and he's been to Williamsburg. They hadn't seen each other for five years, since her sister Marky and his brother George's wedding; but when they did, sparks flew!

Jimbo is now Dr. James Howell O'Callaghan serving an internship at the Naval Hospital in Portsmouth, Virginia. He thinks he is worked to death and has managed to slip up to Williamsburg only once. He won't be home until December twenty-ninth.

Karen is singing with a group of three guys and three gals on the West Coast of California. They have been all the way to South Dakota twice, for bookings. We keep hoping she'll come on home, but the lure is still too strong. Marky and George moved back to Atlanta from Key West in July to start George's residency at Grady Hospital. We were thrilled to have them and Lisa with us until they found a house. Lisa is a precious two-year-old who can move everything in this house in ten minutes. She knows all her letters, and Marky is teaching her to read! Mother and Marnie enjoy them too.

As this hectic year closes, we take note of our blessings, chief among which are our family and wonderful friends. We celebrate with you this joyous Christmas and pray God's blessings on you and yours throughout the year!

Jim, Mary and family

Commentary — 1970

Karen joined a group of singers, entertaining at supper clubs and resort areas. It wasn't long until she pared down to one partner, Gary Edgington. Her heart was still conservative, though her lifestyle was anything but conventional for a Southern belle. Despite the mores of the entertainment world and the "new morality," which is nothing more than acceptance of the old immorality, Mary didn't worry about Karen, for Karen knew who she was in Christ Jesus and wouldn't consider bending His pattern to accommodate to the world's propagated views. They were called by some "the Billy Graham duo" because they let it be known they expected separate quarters. She and Gary were eventually to make several trips to the Far East with the USO, as well as a six-week stint in Europe. They ended up relocating Gary's mother from Monterey, California, to Naples, Florida, where Gary himself eventually settled.

Traveling from a tour of duty in Vietnam, through Atlanta, to Fort Knox, Bill MacNabb and Cindy got "reacquainted" after their initial meeting at the wedding five years before. Romance was in the air. They took Lisa with them to Newnan to visit Ella MacNabb (Bill and George's mother and Lisa's other grandmother). A friend at George's said, "Here comes a couple with a baby." George informed him, "The man is my brother, the girl is Marky's sister, and the baby is ours."

Update — 1998

How fast the leaven of godlessness and immorality worked its way into American culture! Except for those with a strong biblical heritage and commitment, the gross ways of "the world" were the standard, exploited by every greedy merchant of evil. The barrage of filth wore down the natural idealism of youth, and peer pressure exceeded lifeless, uninspired Sunday school upbringing. Fighting a war that was never intended to be won, in jungles halfway around the world, destroyed the morale and patriotic fervor of our young fighting men. They returned home, hanging their heads from the uselessness of it all, seemingly bearing shame rather than being hailed as heroes! America was being undermined. The Church needed reviving that it might give meaning and purpose to the chaos around the world. Satan is trying to bring the world back to the condition of *tohu* and *bohu* (Hebrew for "without form" and "void"), with Darkness on the face of the deep (Genesis 1:2). But God said, *"Let there be Light,"* and Light was! He still is! May the Church live up to its calling to be Light and extinguish the Darkness!

Interim Letter

Naples, Florida
September 27, 1971

Greetings to Kith and Kin, far and wide!

    Over thirty years ago Jim lured me on a matrimonial journey to Florida with promises of a little white cottage on a lake so that all we had to do was reach our hands out the window and pluck oranges for breakfast. There have been many cottages in the meantime, along with many "fruitful" events of the intervening years, but we have come back to Florida to claim our dream!

    We feel so blessed we don't even mind tackling the grass that seems to grow an inch a day during the rainy season, nor the mole crickets that are tunneling through the yard, nor the other little tropical dividends that go with Florida and make us realize our little paradise is on Earth and this isn't really Heaven. Our "cottage" is on the circle of a dead-end street, backing on a canal that is just off Naples Bay and excellent fishing grounds. (We dined on mangrove snapper and red fish tonight that Jim caught yesterday.) We are seven blocks from the Gulf, just a nice bike ride, one of the more popular modes of transportation in this sea-level town. (Naples is where you'd better be careful, or you'll get run over by a little old man on a tricycle!)

    Our oranges have turned out to be limes, which suits us just right. The house is U-shaped, around a lovely pool that miraculously stays almost chilly even in the hottest weather. We hope it will be as enticingly warm in the winter. It was built and occupied for one year by an architect, so it has many surprise features we couldn't have thought of had we tried to build our own dream house. Closet space is fantastic, an urgent requirement where there is no attic or basement, since we are moving from our large house with terrace apartment, plus our King's Port Club apartment here. The three bedrooms flank the large entry hall and living room on the right; the pool is in the center and the laundry, a fourth bedroom or small study, dining room, kitchen and family room are on the left. The master bath is a "garden bath," but the vines will have to grow a lot thicker before I take down the shower curtains I bought.

Mary M. O'Callaghan

Please accept this "interim report" as a personal letter, since we are still chin-deep in boxes in the garage, which I haven't unpacked because I don't know where I can put it all. Besides, this way I can write everyone at once, without deciding who should come first. I overtaxed my brain in Atlanta trying to figure out what to discard of twenty years' accumulation of eight pack rats, and my decision-maker is still sprained. For instance, the movers asked me if I had bricks in a couple of the particularly heavy, huge boxes, and I had to confess they were seashells from Florida that I had diligently carried to Atlanta over the years. Well, you know I couldn't leave them in Atlanta!

It seems strange living on a street where half of the owners are absentee residents. When I walk Rafferty at night, it is like strolling on a dark country road, with stars coming right down to the ground and crickets and cicadas singing all around while tree toads serenade each other with the most unusual sounds. The neighbors who are here now are lovely, and it is exciting meeting and making new friends. (But not as exciting as keeping up with the old, so do keep in touch with us!) Wendy and Laurie are in split sessions, so that Wendy leaves at 6:30 AM to ride her bike the five blocks to catch the free county bus. She gets out at noon, and Laurie leaves at 11:30 AM and gets home at 6:00 PM. They have found it is not as hard to make new friends as they first feared. Wendy has decided she would like to go to summer school, take the few courses she needs to graduate, and head to college next year. Since they don't offer summer school here, she'll live in with Cindy in Atlanta, and finish there.

Naples offers a very popular adult education program, taught by various leaders in their field, so I signed up for typing on Wednesday nights and found out I can also take an art course on Monday morning from a young Italian artist whose studio is near our house. You can't beat a three-hour, fifteen-week course for two dollars a course, can you? I'm just sorry I didn't have time to take jiffy gourmet cooking, and sculpting, but maybe next semester. I had already paid twenty-five dollars to the "Y" for a six-week course in tole painting, before I discovered this other bonanza.

We are visiting churches before we decide where to make our new church home. Besides two Presbyterian, we have attended Methodist, Episcopal and Lutheran churches. Jim loves McCormick & Company, of which he is now a Vice President. He has a beautiful office in a lovely new mall on Gulf Shore Boulevard overlooking Lowdermilk Park and the beach. If things get dull, he can stroll

The Government Shall Be Upon Whose Shoulder?

across the street and look for the two alligators that have taken up residence in the pond. Those who know Jim best will marvel with me that he has come home several times in the middle of the day to cut the grass, take a plunge in the pool, grab some lunch, don his clothes again and head back to manage the office. Such is life in the summer in a little resort town out of season!

Marky, George and Lisa expect to get down here in October for his two-week vacation, and bring Mother with them. We are hoping Mother will decide to take up residence with us on a temporary, if not permanent, basis.

Karen has just returned to California from her forty-five-day hospital tour for the USO in Japan, Korea, Okinawa, Guam and the Philippines. She was happy but exhausted when she called. Jimbo sent us some snapshots from Rota, Spain, his Navy assignment. He likes it better than he did at first. His aim now is to get ahead in his finances (a tough job for him) so he can travel Europe when he gets the chance. Bill MacNabb will finish his service at Fort Knox the middle of November, and he and Cindy haven't definitely decided where they will go from there. Anyone know of a golden opportunity for a good journalist? Our girls want to spend Christmas in Atlanta with Lisa, so we'll be up that way then.

Do let us hear from all of you. We love and miss you.

        The Neapolitans
        Mary, Jim et al.

Christmas Newsletter — 1971

The last hours of November are slipping into the past, and the world around us seems gaily attuned to a tropical Christmas message of love and worship. From a front-row seat in a shady corner of our backyard we watch and become a part of the timeless drama. Thousands of minnows flash in the hot afternoon sun, seemingly unmindful of the playful mullet splashing in the canal like so many schoolchildren, bursting heavenward every few seconds. A white egret majestically lifts one yellow foot and then the other in his regal stroll along the seawall of a neighbor across the canal, as if proudly flaunting ownership of all he surveys. Seagulls circle in the crystal blue above, accenting with their black-tipped wings the fluffs of white clouds lazily pushed along by a seaward breeze. One toss of a choice morsel into the air creates a veritable seagull circus, with performers magically appearing from out of nowhere, chorusing their raucous requests for more. A brown butterfly samples the sweet goodness of delicate yellow blossoms on a lacy tree next door, and bright bursts of flame-colored blossoms contrast with the delicate pink hibiscus in our own yard. Tiny green limes swell proudly, nestled among the leaves of our little lime tree, announcing their miracle of fruition.

As if on cue, five wild ducks drop into the canal arena to preen and perform before exiting for other stages. A young chameleon darts up and down the flame vine that grows across our back fence, adorned in his most brilliant chartreuse. Honeybees work busily among the white Florida jasmine blossoms in the corner. A few sandy seashells by the back door declare the proximity of the powdery white beach and Gulf, and God's special creation there. Behind the wooden gate of our little board-fenced garden bath, two proud purple stalks of orchids, among the other plants, sway their contentment to have returned to their native Florida after a twenty-year sojourn in Atlanta.

High overhead, the whine of a jet reminds us that man, too, soars and reaches up to His God. And Christmas reminds us that God reaches down to His own, in His very special loving way. What a symphony of joy!

It is the eternal joy that allows one to smile through the tears of grief at the loss of a beloved brother and aunt. It is the joy that assures one of Paradise with promised delights far exceeding the delights of our little earthbound paradises. It

The Government Shall Be Upon Whose Shoulder?

is the joy of music and beauty and loveliness and love. It is the joy of forgiving and forgetting. It is the joy of sharing and sacrificing. It is the joy of living. This is God's joy, given for all to share, even as we share Emmanuel, "God with us."

Unlike the wild ducks, we are content to stay in our little paradise in Naples. Only seven blocks away the sun puts on an incomparable nightly display of fireworks as it slips in spectacular splendor beyond the far reaches of the blue Gulf. The shell-laden beaches, laced with sea oats on one edge and skimming sandpipers on the other, are a constantly changing source of pleasure.

In less than ten minutes, from our back dock, we can cast our lines into fish-infested waters. Such proximity affords Jim opportunities before and after work (and sometimes in between for special visitors!). We came down in June for Jim to manage the new branch of McCormick & Company, a Chicago-based investment firm, of which he is now a Vice President and Director. We sold our house in Atlanta and our apartment here and found a house just perfect for us and ours.

Wendy has just started a job in a bookstore to fill her hours and pocketbook. She'll go to summer school in Atlanta, graduate and head to college without a senior year. That will give us a three-year spread of college before Laurie flies the coop to leave the nest empty. We miss Marky and George and watching Lisa grow up, as well as our many friends in Atlanta. But who would swap the peace and charm of village life, where we can bicycle all over town, for the crush and noise of Atlanta traffic? Not us!

Last spring we busied with preparations for Cindy's wedding in the historic Christopher Wren Chapel on her campus in Williamsburg, to become our second Mrs. MacNabb. Our former pastor, Dr. Fred Stair, left his duties as President of the seminary in Richmond long enough to tie the knot. They set up housekeeping at Fort Knox and even entertained some of us home folks in the rolling hills of Kentucky before Bill became a civilian once again in November. We wondered if there really was any gold left at Fort Knox! Bill put his journalistic skills to work at the Atlanta newspapers. Lacking a teaching prospect, Cindy went to work at Dealers Supply, the heating and air-conditioning company Jim started.

Jimbo was assigned to the Naval Hospital at Rota, Spain, after his internship at Portsmouth, Virginia. He reports that bullfights are gory, sanitation is terrible in Spain, and nothing is quite as nice as Naples, Florida! Karen is still in Monterey, California, singing for her bread and butter, and ecstatically happy taking classes at the college, practicing, sharing her faith, and creating compo-

Mary M. O'Callaghan

sitions and ceramics. She says they pack a full house where they work in Monterey.

We wish you all the same bounty of blessings that we enjoy, and even more, as we enter this happy season of rejoicing. Jesus is born! He is Lord! He's coming back for a Bride prepared to meet Him in the air! Hallelujah!

Looking Back From 1998

Living in the cocoon of the "good life" in America, one hardly bothers to address the political situation, other than to complain about the taxes or waste or ineptitude in government, or the scandals and ever-lowering morals in society. Complaints are generally offered without intent to roll up the sleeves and sacrifice for the cause. It is those with a cause, those with nothing to lose and everything to gain, who enter the fray to control matters.

There is an ancient archenemy of everything godly and righteous. He is known as Satan, the adversary, the father of lies, the ruler of this world, the prince of the power of the air, the great dragon, the accuser of the brethren, the tempter, the devil. He was defeated at Calvary and stripped of his authority, but his power has not yet been withdrawn. God is using him to separate the wheat from the chaff. He disguises himself as an angel of light, which brings to light the hidden motives in men's hearts. Men with a cause listen to his voice, and act. The overriding cause is world domination. The motivation is lust for power. The strength of it is pride, the very cause of Satan's downfall. Men are listening, conspiring, and working stealthily. But God is on the throne!

Christmas Newsletter — 1972

For unto you is born a Saviour, the Christ, the Messiah, Lord of Lords, King of Kings, the Anointed One, Wonderful Counselor, Mighty God, Everlasting Father, Prince of Peace, the Word, Son of the Most High, Son of the Living God, Son of Man, Only Begotten, Firstborn, High Priest, Prophet, Cornerstone, Servant, Elder Brother, Redeemer, Last Adam, Messenger, Lamb of God, Light of the World, the Way, the Truth, the Resurrection and the Life, Your Salvation, Deliverer, Helper, Separator, the Door, the Good Shepherd, the True Vine, Bread of Life, Living Water, Alpha and Omega, Holy One, One with the Father, the Great Physician, Interpreter, Teacher, Perfect Revelation, I AM, Jesus, Branch, Emmanuel — God With Us, Love! Can we do less than join the angelic Hallelujah Chorus in praise of and thanksgiving for such a gift?!

Our first Christmas as Neapolitans last year we enjoyed the preening ducks, the stately egrets, the soaring gulls, the frolicking fish, the shy chameleons, the bold and dainty blossoms, the fleeting clouds, the exquisite shells, the crystal-bright stars and all the joyous Christmas kaleidoscope of nature. A year later, we still think Naples is a little corner of paradise. Perhaps the gentle dove settling in the tree next to me is symbolic of that affirmation!

The O'Callaghan family continues to be blessed with health, happiness and lots of love. Marky, George and Lisa are finalizing house plans for their wooded hillside lot in Newnan, Georgia. After this fellowship year at Emory Hospital, George can finally start practicing in that beautiful clinic that awaits him. Cindy and Bill will sorely miss their regular badminton games and suppers with them. Bill still writes for the *Atlanta Constitution*, and Cindy is becoming a jill-of-all-trades at Dealers Supply.

Jimbo was ordered to the Marine Supply Center in Albany, Georgia, at his request, after a lonely year in Spain. He came through Atlanta on his way to Naples, met Leah Rutledge, went back to Atlanta, and married her even before reporting to Albany! They are very happily situated in a married officers' duplex on the lovely base there, and he works with two other doctors in the dispensary. After his Navy duty he would like to do a specialty residency and settle in Naples.

Mary M. O'Callaghan

Karen and her partner, Gary, had a USO tour of Vietnam and Thailand and wrenched our hearts with her snapshots of the orphan babies there. Their needs are so great; there are not enough attendants to keep the flies brushed off them or to touch them lovingly. When the Americans leave, what little they have will probably cease. She and Gary came to Atlanta to job hunt but will leave on December 20 for another USO tour of Vietnam. We are consoled to know they will carry some Christmas joy to the boys still over there and to her Vietnamese orphanage. At least we will see her briefly in Atlanta before they take off.

Wendy reported to Vanderbilt University as a freshman ten days after graduating from summer school. She was too tired and uninspired to even shop for clothes! Blessed with a darling roommate and many friends, she loves "Vandy." Marky, Lisa and I certainly enjoyed taking her to Nashville and visiting all the aunts and cousins there. Both of Jim's parents were from Nashville.

This year Laurie goes to school from 10:00 AM to 5:25 PM. She started a job setting tables at the Beach Club Hotel (where we had spent several vacations in May with MayMa and Aunt "Ceal" during the girls' early school years). Yep, I'm her chauffeur in Dad's Cadillac!

Helen Blair came from Vienna, Georgia, to grace the McCormick & Company reception desk, so we've had a great time getting her settled. She tried it and she liked it, so she's in a new apartment now and we are rounding up furnishings. She had been our neighbor in Atlanta.

Mother has stayed with us, at Jim's invitation, and loves all the comings and goings. She heads out whenever we do, be it to Atlanta or just to dinner! Jim is Captain of our fleet of two boats. You have to have two because one is always in repair at the marina! Fishing is not great right now but he valiantly perseveres. McCormick is planning a big open house this weekend to show off their beautiful newly enlarged quarters. Jim loves it and still manages to squeeze in a golf game or two a week.

Karen came to Naples for a visit and located Charisma Chapel for us. We had been visiting churches for a year, without settling on one to join. I know that was God's plan, for I would never have ventured nine miles up the highway in little bitty Naples if I had been settled in a church home! Jim liked the Episcopal church but his lifelong Presbyterian membership kept him from committing to join it. Naples is distinctly a resort town, with the population tripling during "the season," Thanksgiving through Easter. Many people occupy their gorgeous homes for only three

The Government Shall Be Upon Whose Shoulder?

months out of the year, so churches expect fluctuating memberships. I had volunteered to work with the youth at the Episcopal church, so one day every week during the school year about ten girls meet at our house for fellowship and Bible study. I would go to early service there with Jim, and then Mom, Laurie and I would dash up to Charisma Chapel. I had told the rector I was looking for a church with power — not even knowing what to call it, but I knew when I had found it! It's real!

Our wish for you this New Year is that you claim the gift of Christmas as your own! Then we know you will have a Happy New Year.

Mary, Jim and all the gang

O'Callaghan Christmas Greetings — 1973

The reflection of the blueberry sherbet sky with whipped cream clouds ripples in the waters of our canal. The magnificent beauty of God's creation is punctuated by the shrill whistle of jets overhead, winging into our little tropical paradise the annual "snowbird" migration. Man is always seeking a portion of ultimate perfection, and what he finds is change and aging — that is, until Christmas comes into his heart and consumes his own being with a changeless, infinite love! This divine and everlasting love was ordained before creation and brought to fruition in one brief, magnificent, sinless life from Christmas to Calvary, and beyond! Love must give. In response, we O'Callaghans wrap up our love with a tropical bow to send to each of you this Christmas.

This is the first Christmas our family has spent away from Atlanta. Jimbo will be there with the Rutledges, and Marky will have her first Christmas in Newnan (forty miles from Atlanta) while we pretend a tropical Christmas is the norm for us. Karen, Cindy and Bill, Wendy, Laurie, Mother, Gary and Virginia Edgington and Helen Blair will help us decorate the tree, join in carols accompanied by the "O'C" recorder trio, and spread the festive table. Movie cameras will roll so that we might share the "oohs and aahs" and "you-shouldn't-have; what-is-it's?" with our family up "north." We have planned a handmade Christmas this year, so we are frantically making rather than frantically buying!

In rapid succession, this year Cindy and Bill bought a house near Marky and George in Atlanta; Bill called Jim to ask about a possible job at Dealers Supply, where Cindy was working; Jim informed them he was resigning from McCormick, so why not come to Naples and seek their fortune here. Bill joined Dealers to learn the air-conditioning business, turned over their month-old house to new owners, came to Naples to get licensed, and Florida Comfort Corporation was born. Then they discovered that is not all that is to be born! There will be a new little Neapolitan in March 1974! In May of this year Amy St. Clair MacNabb arrived on her father's birthday, and Lisa is proud to proclaim to the world, "We have a new little sister." They moved to Newnan in August, where George has at long last gone into medical practice.

Jimbo and Leah are still conveniently stationed at Albany, Georgia, hoping the Navy will see fit to release him in July. Karen and Gary are now "struggling"

The Government Shall Be Upon Whose Shoulder?

through a six-week USO tour in Europe! After their last tour in Korea, they plucked up Virginia Edgington (Gary's mother) from Monterey, and now she's working in and loving Naples like us. So far Karen's first love is work, leaving little time for romancing. Wendy is "sophomoring" at "Vandy," a great excuse for me to again visit aunts and cousins in Nashville. At sweet sixteen Laurie is having a great time and is in no hurry to finish school early like Wendy. Jim is momentarily dragging from blood pressure pills — that is, dragging around the golf course about five times a week. Believe it or not, the kids are luring me onto the tennis courts for regular skirmishes. My little Episcopal Girls Fellowship is planning a March trip to the Passion Play in Lake Wales. Mother, Laurie and I (and Karen and Wendy when in town) still find our deepest joy in fellowship at Charisma Chapel.

We wish the abiding love and joy of the One whose birth we celebrate to encompass you all in His fellowship!

Mary, Jim et al., plus Rafferty

It's Christmas Again — 1974!

The symbolic etchings on the sand dollar, with its miniature doves enclosed, and the passionflower vine now bursting in crimson glory on our garden fence delight us in discovering God's signature in His creation. This season we celebrate His crowning gift, a Son begotten for mankind, with His indelible signature of Love. To receive Him is to receive a new name and a new life! Nothing can compare! Joy to the world!

To our mistletoe and Christmas traditions we'll add our second annual tropical Neapolitan-style tradition — caroling by boat through the canals of our neighborhood. With Bill (MacNabb, Cindy's husband) or Ole Dad at the helm, besides Karen, Cindy and Laurie with flute and recorders, Wendy with tambourine or the instrument of her choice, Rafferty howling in my lap as I jingle the bells of Sarna (I'm expert at jingling), and various friends, we'll have several new additions. Little Becky, who surprised Cindy and Bill five weeks early last February 1, can squeak a toy or exercise her talent for squealing lustily. And two new male voices will join the family chorus to pierce the silent night, Reid Barnes from Birmingham and Chris Regas from Jacksonville and Nashville. Karen hadn't seen Reid since her freshman year at Vanderbilt, so it was love at "second" sight for them. Reid graduates from law school this month, so they'll make wedding plans when he gets situated in a job. Chris graduated from "Vandy" in June and started his furniture refinishing business in Nashville, to Wendy's delight. They'd like a summer wedding before she starts her senior year.

Marky and George (MacNabb also) had hoped the whole O'Callaghan-MacNabb clan could "warm" their new house in Newnan by Christmas (it's big enough), but they won't get in it until January. We'll have to share Christmas with Lisa and Amy via home movies. We'll also miss Jimbo and Leah, who have bought a house in Decatur, Georgia. He practices medicine with the Veteran's Administration and Leah teaches grammar school. Laurie is jealous that they can lunch on Sundays with Karen at the Varsity after church at North Avenue Presbyterian. Jim and I and Mother love simple village living in Naples.

Florida Comfort closed its doors October 31, when no relief was seen for the building industry. Bill is now happily using his creative journalistic talents with an advertising firm here, and Cindy is finishing business details at home with

The Government Shall Be Upon Whose Shoulder?

Becky. We all prayed hard that they'd stay in Naples. Mother, at 85, is ever ready to head to Charisma Chapel four or five times a week. This summer she flew to New Orleans to greet her thirteenth great-grandchild, then on to west Texas with Dot and Dick before flying to Columbus, Ohio, to visit her sister, then to my brother Don's in Atlanta. Brother Curtis's family in New Jersey is on the next schedule! I'm preparing to speak at the Moorings Presbyterian Church on the Charismatic Renewal, in which I delight though I'm certainly not an expert.

We cherish this special time of year to send our love to family and friends, and wish you all a joyous Christmas and God's richest blessings in 1975!

Mary, Jim and clanging gang

Christmas 1975 — Naples, Florida

The triumphant reverberations of the "Hallelujah Chorus" resound through the house to proclaim once again the Holy life that has set all earthly events in eternity, with the promise that "He shall reign for ever and ever, King of kings and Lord of lords! Hallelujah! Hallelujah!"

Our big Christmas surprise last year was a call from Marky and George on December 19 that we were blessed with a two-day-old grandson, Benjamin Howell MacNabb! We are looking forward to a Christmas gathering of our clan at the MacNabbs' new house in Newnan. The rafters will ring as Benjie, Amy and Lisa gather around the tree with little cousin Becky MacNabb (Cindy and Bill's), to thrill adoring grandparents, uncles and aunts as they excitedly tackle piles of bright packages. And the oldsters will once again uproariously swap little tokens of love with the traditional, "Thanks a million, you shouldn't have done it. What is it?"

Reid became a legal member of the family in March when Karen became Mrs. Barnes at a home ceremony in the Newnan-MacNabb Manor. Now he is in the legal profession in Birmingham, and Karen is working in an art gallery.

Mother broke her hip in April, but a good "pinup" job enabled her to stroll down the aisle when Wendy and Chris swapped vows and rings on June 14, our thirty-fourth Anniversary. It was an exciting weekend as family and friends poured into town, and we were introduced to each other and to Greek dancing. What fun! Chris even had some kin here from Greece.

Laurie ended high school in a blaze of glory; and when I drove her to Chapel Hill for her freshman year at the University of North Carolina, I managed a "side trip" to Nashville to visit the Regas newlyweds, and family there. Cindy, Becky and Lisa drove there with me to marvel at Wendy's culinary prowess and Chris's gardening skills. He's working for Swift & Company and Wendy is winding up her college career at Vanderbilt. It is mighty lonesome without a chick or child around here, but Laurie prepared us for that by staying on the "go" most of last year!

Cindy and Bill are living in Mother's old house in Atlanta while Bill rejuvenates Dealers Supply Company with some interesting innovations. We do miss them here in Naples, but it is a good move for Dealers Supply. Jimbo and

The Government Shall Be Upon Whose Shoulder?

Leah are still working hard from their Decatur base, and everybody is trying to invent a way to reconcile outgo with income. Somehow the out goes more than the in comes! So what's new! Christmas won't be the same without Jim's brother Bill, but their daughter Becky will keep Kathryn and family busy with her new December 1 son.

Jim still golfs and fishes, and we briskly walk Rafferty to the beach each day (eight blocks). He patiently sits, tethered to a palm frond, while we gather shells and — would you believe — Jim gathers ROCKS! — on the beach. We drink in the beauty of the Gulf and thank God for His grace to us! We've enjoyed seeing some friends during the year and missed seeing others of you. For Auld Lang Syne may we wish each of you a very happy New Year, with prayers that this bicentennial year will be our nation's greatest!

Mary and Jim O'Callaghan

Commentary —
The American Scene — to 1980

Wars and rumors of wars — hot wars and cold wars — have added to the universal feeling and evidence that the world is moving towards a climax (Matthew 24:6). Knowledge has indeed increased (Daniel 12:4). Evil abounds. From high positions in Washington psychics have been consulted concerning our government, and Eastern religions have been introduced to flourish along with witchcraft and Satan worship. Some have come saying, "I am the Christ," and fanaticism has produced the Jonestown tragedy. A Vice President and a President have been deposed, and some in high positions have been jailed. This is not to condone lying or illegalities — our government should be above reproach — but the irony is, this regime followed one that publicly espoused "a right to lie" policy.

By picking and choosing which issues to attack and which to ignore, the media exhibit the power of words to produce death or life (Proverbs 18:21). They create public images without substance and destroy standards and values that have stood the test of time and civilization. We would join the prophet Isaiah *"Woe to them that call evil good, and good evil; that put darkness for light, and light for darkness; that put bitter for sweet, and sweet for bitter!"* (Isaiah 5:20). Truly, deceiving spirits have gone forth to deceive.

We have allowed one woman's atheistic fight to overturn principles upon which this nation was established, even despite the proclamation on every American coin and bill, "In God We Trust." We have allowed the murder of millions of babies to be legalized by the decision of nine men on the Supreme Court. (Would God call them "justices" or "honorable"?) We have tolerated a Congress that has appropriated our tax dollars for such carnage. Pornography is a multi-billion-dollar business, upheld by cries of "censorship" and "antiquated and outmoded values" and "denial of rights" against every effort attempting to stem the tide. A nation that once protected its army, government and families against the abomination of sodomy is being softened not only to accept such but also to legally force such ungodliness to be incorporated into our public and private lives.

The Government Shall Be Upon Whose Shoulder?

As evil abounds, grace superabounds! A new revival of the infilling of the Holy Spirit within Christian believers, starting at the turn of the century and flowering in the charismatic renewal, has made the supernatural natural in the lives of multiplied numbers. Signs and wonders are being wrought worldwide, and a Bride is being prepared for the soon-coming King! His word of love and hope and peace and joy is going out from America to the four corners of the Earth.

God has called His Body, the Church, to be light and salt in the Earth. Has the light gone out and the salt lost its savor? Are we lulled to apathy by a sense of helplessness or hopelessness? Or will we humble ourselves and cry out to God in repentance, turning from our wicked ways to seek His face, and pray for Him to heal our land? (2 Chronicles 7:14). If we truly believe His Word that *"greater is He that is in you, than he that is in the world"* (1 John 4:4) and we submit ourselves wholeheartedly to the God of all creation, being empowered by His Holy Spirit, then the battle is His, and He knows only victory!

Christmas Greetings '76
— The Jim O'Callaghans

When the north wind blows the thermometer down into the forties in tropical Naples, can Christmas be far behind? It also blows in nostalgic memories of icicles and snowballs, holly berries and cedar trimmings, fruit cake and eggnog, times past with loved ones now gone on, and times more recent with a new generation, familiar carols and Christmas bells, mysterious packages and frantic shopping, colorful cards and long-distance calls, midnight services and candle lightings, and precious friends and beloved family, all intermingled to spread Joy to the World, the Lord is Come! And indeed He is! Each year speeds faster than the last, so that we feel almost as if we should hasten this greeting before Christmas '77 catches up with us! Our clan (seventeen plus) will once again accept the MacNabbs' hospitality in Newnan as the focal point of our Christmas celebration, where the tennis court, bridge table and corn popper will see overtime duty.

Laurie is at the University of Colorado in Boulder this sophomore year, just a local call from Wendy and Chris in Denver, where Chris works for CIT Corporation. Those three are enraptured with their mountainous environs and don hiking boots to backpack, bird watch and get close to nature. Laurie may even lure Wendy to the ski slopes before the season is over, which gives cause for envy to a few of us.

Leah and Jimbo are enjoying their new house, closer to where he is practicing at Fort McPherson. Karen and Reid Barnes have settled by degrees into an older house in Birmingham, with a slight assist from Laurie and me riding herd on a couple of paint brushes. Marky and George, with their three young live wires, are not even envious of Cindy and Bill's announcement of a new little sibling for Becky in May.

In celebration of thirty-five years on the sea of matrimony this summer, Jim and I flew to London, crossed at Calais, and drove in stages up to Copenhagen for a two-week cruise aboard the *Royal Viking Star*. Would you believe Jim managed beautifully with nine different currencies in that many countries, not to mention languages? The ship was a delightful hotel for stops in Amsterdam, Hamburg, Helsinki, Leningrad, Stockholm, Visby and back to Copenhagen. One

The Government Shall Be Upon Whose Shoulder?

of the highlights was getting to know Bob and Suzanne Massie, who lectured to us, she on Leningrad and he on his book *Nicholas and Alexandra* and that portion of Russian history. We viewed the movie before visiting Leningrad, and had two lively discussions with them afterwards on impressions and questions about Russia. Jim disliked the stark reality of unsmiling grimness — such a contrast to the magnificent, gorgeously elaborate restorations in their palaces — but I was ever mindful of the many real Christian heroes behind that unseen, but very present, Iron Curtain.

When we took our trip, Laurie flew Mother to Atlanta and settled her happily with my brother Don, where she is surrounded by Don's five married children, three of ours, and too many great-grandchildren to count. She manages to get around with her walker despite the second broken hip suffered just before last Christmas and the broken leg in January that required replacing a pin.

After thirty-five years of a bustling family it is rather strange, though exciting, to settle down to "two and a poodle." Jim busies himself as head of the golf committee at Royal Poinciana Club, and he is serving his final year as President of Aqualane Shores Civic Association. I'm playing at being retired and trying rather unsuccessfully to learn to cook for only two. NO cook books, please! We continue to love Naples, though our many wonderful friends here can't keep us from missing all our "back home" friends and family.

May God bless America as we continue to celebrate this bicentennial year. And may His blessings abound to each one of you and your families in 1977.

Fall Letter — 1977

September 10, 1977

Dear friends and family,

It seemed good to me to advance our annual letter to fall, so our Christmas greeting might be short and sweet, befitting the busy season. Now perhaps some of you won't be too busy to respond in kind! Memories are becoming more important and loved ones more precious with the years.

A few have expressed dismay and confusion as to our six children, their five spouses and now five grandchildren, so I'll run them by, in order of age (though I confess I myself call them by the wrong names at times). Marky (Mary Kathryn) is married to Dr. George MacNabb and they have a large house in Newnan, Georgia, about forty miles southeast of Atlanta. I call it the "MacNabb Motel" because we converge there for family celebrations. Lisa, Amy and Benjie are three of the reasons it is easier for us to go there, plus the enticement of their tennis court that is jointly owned with a neighbor. George is a very busy internist in a very busy clinic in his hometown. Benjie and Amy (two and four) are now in preschool and Lisa in the fourth grade, so Marky has a little breathing time between car pools.

Our only son, Jimbo, is a doctor at Fort McPherson. He and his wife Leah have a lovely home in a new development south of the airport, near his work. They have just closed the hospital at Fort Mac, which reduces their function to something more like a dispensary, which is not quite so satisfying to Dr. Jim.

Karen, our globetrotting, guitar-playing daughter, settled down a couple years ago in Birmingham, Alabama, with her lawyer husband, Reid Barnes, Jr. She works in an art gallery and has developed quite a talent for framing. They are still having a ball — painting, papering and fixing up their house.

We were lucky several years ago to have our Cindy and Bill MacNabb (George's brother) living in Naples when Becky was born. Unfortunately, that was a poor time to launch a heating and air-conditioning business in Naples. They have since settled in Mother's house in Atlanta and Bill is Sales Manager for Dealers Supply Company, the wholesale business Jim started. I was in Atlanta

The Government Shall Be Upon Whose Shoulder?

on the second of June to greet our fifth grandchild. (All five are MacNabbs!) Sandy is as black-headed a little miss as her sister is blonde.

Wendy and Chris Regas moved to Denver after her graduation from "Vandy," where he took a job with CIT Corporation. They loved it there, and Laurie, our youngest, took her sophomore year at the University of Colorado, which was great for all. The day she came home from school, Wendy and Chris were transferred to Casper, Wyoming. Chris travels a good deal and Wendy works in an internist's office. Jim and I hope to sample the fantastic scenery out that way before they are transferred back East.

Laurie has arrived in Regensburg, Germany, along with twenty other students and advisors from the University of Colorado, for her junior year. It is a ten-year-old university with ten thousand students. They will have concentrated language study for six weeks before school starts. She hopes to get home for Christmas. In the spring they have a two-month break. A friend is saving her pennies to go over and travel the youth hostels of Europe with her. Ole Dad and I have designs towards Germany also, Lord willing! Regensburg is an ancient Bavarian town on the Danube, so what's wrong with dreaming of floating on to Vienna for a waltz or two?!

On August 10 my dear little Mother took up permanent residence with her Lord, and I know she is having a marvelous time praising Him face to face. She had lived with my brother Don and Rosie Mees her last year, surrounded by grandchildren and great-grandchildren. Despite those two broken hips and broken leg, she miraculously seemed to suffer no pain. We can only rejoice.

Brother Curtis and Colette moved to Florida briefly, but the climate didn't agree with Colette and they went to Atlanta. My cousin Miriam and Edgar Bauer liked wintering in Naples so much that they sold their house in Baltimore and bought a condominium to share our Neopolitan delights.

Jim surprised me by taking a real estate course while Laurie and I were in Atlanta and Birmingham after Mother's funeral. He is still on the board of our club and is an elder in the Presbyterian Church, but he is ready to retire from retirement!

I dusted off my nearly forgotten French last spring and joined my sister Dot and Dick Kendrick for a spring-break trip to Paris. For six years Dot has sponsored a trip for her French students. Paris is indeed an enchanting city, and I can see why they like to keep going back.

Mary M. O'Callaghan

I'm still involved in church activities. One of my pet loves is a little orphanage and clinic in Haiti started by Doris and Don Peavey. They are real angels of mercy to live in that poverty-stricken land, filled with witchcraft, voodoo, ignorance, starvation and civil unrest. God will reward them!

Let us hear from you and keep this conversation from being one-sided. The welcome mat is out for any who will come our way.

Love,
Mary and Jim

Christmas Blessings — 1978;
Aloft Over Wyoming

December 8, 1978

What a glorious winter wonderland! Thirty-seven thousand feet beneath me, the Earth snuggles under a huge white patchwork quilt with ribbonlike rivulets embroidering the geometric designs with their tree-lined featherstitching. From this God's-eye view of Earth, with my face still tingling from the wind-driven snow, it is easy to slip into the Christmas spirit. My mind's eye carries me to a stable where a young girl has just experienced the pain and joy of bringing a little life into the world, cradling Him in the feeding trough of the animals. Quite a contrast to the comforting safety of the hospital in Casper, Wyoming, where our precious newly-born grandchild was swaddled in controlled humidity, sterility and temperature. The wonder and joy of little Anastasia Alexandra Regas, nine pounds two ounces, born December 4, the first child of Wendy and Chris Regas, punctuate the preciousness of that Holy birth almost two thousand years ago. They chose the name "Anastasia," which takes us from Christmas to Easter, for it means "resurrection"!

After her junior year in Regensburg, Germany, in the University of Colorado program, Laurie returned to the University of North Carolina her senior year to get her degree. She joined us in Casper during her Thanksgiving break from Chapel Hill to await the expected November 23 arrival, but Anastasia had her own schedule. At least Laurie enjoyed a visit with her Colorado friends. A beautiful fresh snowfall afforded her and Chris a day of cross-country skiing, and at nine months and holding, Wendy even gave me a lesson. She and Chris will miss the great Western outdoors when CIT transfers them in January to Jacksonville, his hometown. Jacksonville is a great stopping place between Atlanta and Naples, so they will, no doubt, entertain many a traveling baby sitter!

As I wing southward, the landscape is throwing off its white quilt to expose colorful patches and trees, once again green. From nineteen degrees below in Casper, I'm heading to record high in the eighties in Naples. From the Mile-High City, I'm dropping to our little town at sea level. From scarves and boots and crackling fires I'll be changing to shorts and sandals and air-conditioning.

Mary M. O'Callaghan

In Atlanta, Jimbo and Leah were also playing the waiting game. Sarah finally arrived on December 10, in time to hang her little Christmas stocking in Newnan with the other grandchildren's. The Barneses won't qualify to hang a wee stocking until the end of April. The clan doth grow, and seventeen of us will fill the "Newnan-MacNabb Hostel" with songs and cheer and much rollicking laughter. Jesus came to show us what "family" really is, as we thank our Father for His Love poured out! The celebration will continue after Christmas when Lisa, Amy and Karen come to Naples to indulge in Florida delights with us. Wendy and Chris will introduce Anastasia to the Regas branch in Jacksonville on Christmas night. When Chris goes back to Casper, to oversee moving, we expect Wendy to bring Anastasia to Naples for "show-and-tell."

In the midst of all our movings around, please know that our thoughts and love remain constant towards our friends and family, and we rejoice once again to be able to wish you a very special and Christ-filled Christmas, with every possible blessing in 1979!

Mary and Jim O'Callaghan

Christmas Greetings from the O'Callaghans in Naples — 1979

From our own front door in Naples I recently was thrilled to behold a perfect Christmas card scene! The palm trees were silhouetted against the darkening rosy afterglow of sunset and one lone star twinkled ever brighter in close communion with a brand new sliver of a moon. God's pageantry, though daily rehearsed, never loses the freshness of its awe-inspiring wonder! In contrast, the daytime scene of bathing-suit-clad enthusiasts, encumbered with beach chairs and buckets, strolling or biking to and from the Gulf seems to belie the approaching holiday season. But glory be! December rolled in with a sudden drop in temperature, and now "it's beginning to feel a lot like Christmas."

Once again we were blessed to celebrate the birth, on May 1, of grandchild number eight, Danielle Barnes, a little black-haired, blue-eyed doll of Karen and Reid in Birmingham. Benjie MacNabb remains the lone boy in the crowd, a feeling his Uncle Jimbo knows well, surrounded by five sisters!

Once again we celebrated a college graduation as Laurie, the last of our six, donned cap and gown adorned with Phi Beta Kappa key and waved good-bye to the University of North Carolina at Chapel Hill. At least that is what we thought until a certain young North Carolina dental student appeared as an irresistible force, hopefully attracting her back to the spot she had so recently vacated.

Once again we are thankful for a year of health, wealth (of family if not of fleeting dollars) and happiness. We swapped six weeks of our unusually hot summer for a vacation at Sugar Mountain, North Carolina, where various family and friends of Laurie's joined us to hike the mountains, pick wild blackberries and blueberries, compete on the alpine slide, and vie for yahtzee and tennis championships.

In October, after taking over as President of our Women's Aglow chapter, I joined twenty-three hundred women from all over the world in Houston for the Women's Aglow Fellowship International Leadership Conference. That's an imposing name for an imposing organization of charismatic women from every denomination and every continent. As the Holy Spirit moves throughout the Earth in a mighty and marvelous way, it is exciting to be in the middle of it, witnessing and sharing His wondrous ways!

Mary M. O'Callaghan

Once again the O'Callaghan clan will celebrate the sacred birth in Newnan, Georgia. And once again we count our friends and family as our greatest earthly blessings. We regret that we have seen fewer and fewer of you, especially on our limited excursions to Atlanta; I'm convinced no one stays at home there! As we address each card, know that our thoughts and love are flowing out to you, and our sincerest wish for you all is that you know in a new dimension and enjoy in a new fullness the One whose birth we now celebrate!

HALLELUJAH!

Commentary — 1998

When young King Solomon dedicated the temple he had built for the Lord's Name, he reminded the Lord of His promises to his father David. He asked the Lord to hear the prayers of His people and to forgive their sins. *"If Your people Israel are defeated before an enemy because they have sinned against You... when the heavens are shut up and there is no rain because they have sinned against You... when there is famine in the land, pestilence or blight or mildew, locusts or grasshoppers, when their enemies besiege them in the land of their cities... then hear from heaven Your dwelling place, and forgive, and give to everyone according to all his ways... **that they may fear You,** to walk in Your ways..."* (selected verses from 2 Chronicles 6:17-31, NKJV).

After the marvelous dedicatory celebration, Solomon sent the people home. Then the Lord appeared to him by night and said, *"I have heard your prayer ... when I shut up heaven and there is no rain, or command the locusts to devour the land, or send pestilence among My people, if My people who are called by My name will humble themselves, and pray and seek My face, and turn from their wicked ways, then I will hear from heaven, and will forgive their sin and heal their land"* (2 Chronicles 7:12-14, NKJV).

If:

    1. God's people humble themselves and pray
    2. They seek His face
    3. They turn from their wicked ways

Then:

    1. He will hear from heaven
    2. He will forgive their sin
    3. He will heal their land

Christians are grafted into Israel like wild olive branches into the natural olive tree. Their warnings are ours, through Jesus the Messiah, just as surely as are their promises. If we are defeated before an enemy, or if there is no rain, or if there is famine, or pestilence, or locusts or grasshoppers, or if we are besieged because we have sinned, then the above requirements will bring the above results, **that we may fear HIM.**

Mary M. O'Callaghan

"The fear of the LORD *is to hate evil"* (Proverbs 8:13).
"The fear of the LORD *is the beginning of wisdom"* (Psalm 111:10).
"The fear of the LORD *is the beginning of knowledge"* (Proverbs 1:7).
"The fear of the LORD *prolongs life"* (Proverbs 10:27, NASB).
"The fear of the LORD *is a fountain of life"* (Proverbs 14:27).
"The fear of the LORD *is the instruction of wisdom"* (Proverbs 15:33).
"By the fear of the LORD *men depart from evil"* (Proverbs 16:6b).

Our national pride must lead God's people to national humility as we identify with the sins of our nation. There is a dearth of the fear of the Lord in America because there is a dearth of the fear of the Lord in the Church. No longer is sin being called sin, so there is no need for repentance. If there is no need for repentance, is there a need for God? Can man be his own God, as the New Age imagines? Will the Lord heal our land as long as we deny Him in our public arena?" Is our light darkness? Has our salt lost its savor?

GOD IS STILL ON THE THRONE!!!

Christmas Greetings from the O'Callaghans — 1980

Two shepherds herding their scattered flock from the green valley up the rocky hillside delighted me as I watched from my hotel window in Jerusalem. The sheep meandered slowly up the ascent, testing the barren hill for bits of edibles while the goats frolicked over the rocks. Sunset splashed across the late afternoon sky, putting the valley to rest under a shadowy blanket. The herd, now resembling moving stones on the stony landscape, disappeared in the twilight at the crest. How beautifully reminiscent of the scene almost two thousand years ago when the angels announced to humble shepherds the advent of the Messiah! As I reaffirmed Jesus as Lord of my life, the pastoral silence was broken by the strange sounds of a rival call to worship from a minaret on a distant hill. In this land in which God chose His Name to dwell, I was reminded that all eternity hinges on one's decision about Jesus. O little town of Bethlehem! O Jerusalem, Jerusalem!

On March 1 in Newnan, Georgia, Jim gave away his fifth and last daughter, Laurie, to Gene Modlin, with tears of sadness for the "empty nest" and of joy for another fine son in the family. Gene passed muster by all prospective in-laws with flying colors and is now passing muster on exams in his junior year in dental school at Chapel Hill. We'll all gather at Marky and George's in Newnan right after Christmas, except for Wendy and Chris, who are expecting another wee one in mid-January. We'll celebrate together a day late to allow for beginning Christmas traditions in each growing family.

In March, Karen and Reid will bless Danielle with a sibling in Birmingham, and Cindy and Bill MacNabb will continue the population explosion in April in Atlanta. With seven granddaughters and only one grandson, Chris is praying, "Lord, raise up an army!"

I trust these three babies are properly scheduled between my Women's Aglow meetings, so I can preside at all of them! Even Jim is enjoying hosting our wonderful monthly Aglow speakers overnight, since our meetings are in the morning, but he won't hazard attending. Our Vice President and I went to Jerusalem in November for the Aglow International Convention. We toured Israel and had a quickie tour of Rome afterwards on our return home.

Mary M. O'Callaghan

The void left by Rafferty's death last spring has been rambunctiously filled by Skipper, a two-pound, four-month-old, cream poodle with apricot ears. His puppy antics rule the household, and Jim once more has someone to spoil. Though it was too hot for much golf this summer, gentleman farmer Jim gathered in avocados, bananas, guavas, mangoes, coconuts and limes — an amazing harvest for our small yard.

What an election! After licking our wounds for so many years, I must confess it was fun licking our chops. With Reagan in, let's aim now for two years hence and finish cleaning up the mess.

We love to keep in touch with you, even if it's only once a year, so please share your news with us. We send our love wrapped in a big red ribbon to each of you and wish you and yours God's best in 1981!

Merry Christmas '81,
from the Neapolitan O'Callaghan Clan

JOY, JOY, JOY!!! That's our '81 holiday wish to kith and kin all over the land! And that's what we experienced!

January 3 ushered in our first little JOY of the year in Jacksonville, Meredith Kathryn Regas, second daughter of Wendy and Chris. Anastasia was disappointed that Skipper stayed in Naples with Papa when I flew up to be an extra pair of hands and eyes. Karen expected our second little JOY on March 20 in Birmingham, so I headed north again via Jacksonville and Atlanta. I had a full week in Birmingham for Danielle to get used to me before Reid Boylston Barnes IV (Ryon) belatedly put in his appearance on March 30 (which proves the O'Callaghan clan *can* produce boys). Ryon's timing brought anxious calls from Cindy in Atlanta expecting her third and expecting Mom to oversee Becky and Sandy. Emily Cotter MacNabb arrived April 7 — our third and last little JOY of the year, to complete our family circle at twenty-five. This was all sandwiched in between my monthly Women's Aglow responsibilities, which included the pleasure of hosting our wonderful speakers in our home.

The great thing about living in a resort town is that your family loves to visit, not just from "duty." With instant fishing as well as boating from the back dock, an easy bike ride to the beach to sun and splash and seek shells, golf courses and tennis courts available at our pleasure, and marvelous food at the Royal Poinciana Club, plus wonderful public restaurants, we never had to urge the family to spend their two-week vacations with us!

Cindy (MacNabb) and her three girls flew in from Atlanta on June 14 to help Jim and me celebrate our Fortieth Anniversary. Bill drove down a little later. Before Marky (MacNabb) drove down July 6 with Lisa, a friend, Amy and Benjie, and I flew out to St. Louis for the Annual World Convention of the End-Time Handmaidens and Servants. That's a marvelous charismatic group with missionaries all over the world, founded by Gwen Shaw, a missionary to China and the nations. It started out just for women intercessors and workers but so many pastors and men wanted to be a part of it, and younger children, that it has become a family commitment. Marky and the kids picked up George at the Miami airport to drive to Key West before finishing their visit in Naples. They wanted to show them where they were stationed for three years and where Lisa was born.

Mary M. O'Callaghan

Laurie (Modlin) and Gene came down and painted half the inside of the house in mid-August before Laurie was to be in a friend's wedding here in Naples. Karen and Reid planned their visit to coincide, stopping in Jacksonville a couple of days with the Regases. Wendy found out Chris had to go out of town, so she piled into the car with the Barneses — three adults and four children! We were wall-to-wall bathing suits, buckets and shovels, card tables, nursing babies, sleeping bags and fun! All got here but Jimbo; he can't stand the heat. At least his wife Leah and Sarah drove down with Cindy and her girls to keep Ole Dad company one of the three weeks in October that I was in Israel. I went with the End-Time Handmaidens and stayed on the Mount of Olives overlooking the old city of Jerusalem. That is the usual panoramic view you see, with the golden Dome of the Rock in the center. From the back of the hotel we could see the sun reflecting from the Dead Sea way down in the distance. We toured "from Dan to Beersheba" after our convention, and four of us from Florida stayed on a kibbutz a couple days before returning to Jerusalem for a Prayer and Fasting Conference, with many Koreans.

There is an unusual magnetic attraction to Israel — strangely like coming home to roots! My mother's name, Beulah, in Hebrew means "married." Now I can better understand why they call it "Beulah land"; it is as if those who love God are made one with the land which He chose above all other places in the Earth as His special habitation! God is very zealous for and jealous of His land, like a husband for a wife He loves! Perhaps it is because Messiah Jesus, our soon-coming Bridegroom, was born and lived there and will be returning there!

Jesus is the reason for all the JOY that we have as we wrap gifts and mail cards, nostalgically remembering friends and Christmases past, and overflowing with love and best wishes for you all!

Mary and Jim and Skipper, too

O'Callaghan Christmas Greetings, '82

Do you know HIM, this One whose birth we celebrate each December 25, the Word made flesh to dwell among us and within us? HE came and suffered and died that HE might impart to us the precious gift of eternal life with HIM! What love! What grace! What joy! What peace!

Having retired from retirement, Jim enjoys working at Richardson-Greenshields Securities, Incorporated, for several hours daily. He is diligently studying and analyzing the market, having always been in management heretofore. I'm sure he is becoming quite an expert. Just ask him about gold coins!

My studies tend more to the "gold" in the Word of God, which is a never-ending venture. It might even lead to the depletion of the gold Jim is studying! But Jim has taught me well you can't outgive God!

Jim was a little nervous when I joined a friend in ministry and counseling at the county jail on Sunday evenings for women inmates who might desire Christian fellowship. I confess it was a little unnerving to have to identify myself and wait at the first of a series of doors for someone to push a button to let us through, then close it behind us, to repeat at the next closed door, etc., until we were ushered into a room to wait for the women to be brought in. This was a holding jail until they were sentenced and sent to another facility or freed. I am now associated with Pat Carver International Ministries, so the pace only quickens. Pat, from Mableton, Georgia (a suburb of Atlanta), was one of our Aglow speakers. I was honored when she asked if I would like to become an intercessor with her ministry.

The O'Callaghan clan got by 1982 without a single addition to the family! But Wendy and Chris are looking for their third in Jacksonville in April, and Laurie and Gene Modlin expect to join the ranks of parents in June with our thirteenth grandchild. Gene and a classmate from the University of North Carolina (my old home state) have built a beautiful dental office in an outlying area of Hickory, North Carolina, to start their dental practice. Gene also works with an established practice in Hickory. I made the grand tour up there with one- or two-night stands with each of our other five children, ending up with Karen and family in Birmingham on my way home. Wendy, Chris, Anastasia and Meredith get double duty, coming and going, since Jacksonville is about halfway between Atlanta

Mary M. O'Callaghan

and Naples. Marky canceled plans to drive with me to Hickory, since Lisa and Amy were involved in school homecoming festivities and Benjie with soccer. Instead, the Bill MacNabb girls, Cindy, Becky, Sandy and Emily, with sleeping bags, climbed in with me to admire the glory of fall in the piedmont area of North Carolina and the Modlins' new house. The Lord had graciously delayed His leaf extravaganza, which we relished.

My time with Jimbo, Leah and Sarah coincided with a service in the Rex Community Church, an important part of his life. They still attend North Avenue Presbyterian Church on Sunday mornings. Visits with brothers Don Mees and family in Lawrenceville and Curtis and family in Atlanta were great but brief. Sorry I missed seeing our ol' pals. I'm sure the Georgia Tech Forty-fifth Reunion was a WOW!

We take joy in spanning the miles and years with greetings of love. We can love because He first loved us! Do you know HIM?

A Couple's Marriage Is "A Series of Joys"

By Wendy Regas

(This special feature article was published on October 13, 1983, in *The Florida Times-Union*, Jacksonville, and is reproduced here with the permission of the author, daughter Wendy.)

Two years ago I bought the book *Passages* for twenty-five cents at a garage sale. I thought at the time that I might want a road map for the future, but I've changed my mind. Instead, I've come to relish discovering the trail through the trees.

Of course, there are transitions in our lives and love. I recognize that in our ninth year of marriage Chris and I are traveling a well-paved road, with certain parameters imposed by growing roots and growing children. Our landmarks are more established, but a pioneer exuberance pervades as we take each step together.

I once described our marriage to a friend as "a series of joys." Sure, there are plateaus where the routine seems to go like an endless horizon. But then we turn a corner, meet each other in a new way, and fall right into love again. It's not always at the same time or for the same reason, but one will plunge and take the other with him.

We are best friends. He has encouraged me for any new project or idea. He has stood in line in ten inches of December Wyoming snow to surprise me with the only pottery wheel at the college auction. He has graduated three times from Lamaze instruction and been a superlative coach for our expansion team.

He has gone to the baroque ballet when every other friend has turned me down. He has constantly supported our decision for me to stay home to raise our children, while helping as I grope for new definitions within the traditional forms.

We have been challenged and stimulated by each other's ideas, even when they are usually shared after 11 PM and he would like to be sleeping. We always enjoy each other's company and comfort.

This is not to say there haven't been disappointments. We are pioneers, and we are survivors. Our romance has endured the realization that underneath the long hair and beard that I fell in love with, there lurked a jock. There was also the cold reality for him that some Vanderbilt fans (including his wife) do read art books in the football stands.

We have survived the realization that my idea of relaxation is contemplative; his, physical. It has come as a gradual unfolding that my best friend could be so different, yet so much the same. I can now face the fact that he doesn't like to shop or know that he could play bridge but doesn't want to. (Well, I'm still working on that one!)

Our shared experiences, both good and bad, are a common bond that brings much satisfaction. But the real mortar of our relationship is our faith. We have known since our first meeting in a college pottery class that we were drawn to each other by Someone else. Our commitment to Him brings us full circle to our commitment to each other.

In understanding love and service to God, we are free to meet each other's needs. This personal, stabilizing love brings much peace in an era of fifty-percent divorce rates. We know that ours is the "threefold cord ... not quickly broken"(Ecclesiastes 4:12).

Now, we have stretched the cord a bit at times. Our love has expanded through many avenues. We have shared our anger and channeled it like a cleansing current. Rarely has it overwhelmed us; but then we are careful to respect its potential force.

Mostly we look back on those times as gaps bridged, rather than impasses skirted. Besides, it's comforting to know you have been loved "even when," or to know how deeply you have loved "although."

All this is to say that the real romance we enjoy is not the poetry and roses formula. Rather, it greets us quietly as we check the sleeping children or on a casual night when we are out at a quaint café instead of the rated restaurant.

It is there when we load up the kids for a day of alligators and yellow flies in the Okefenokee Swamp. We feel its warmth when we yawn to face the morning and that special Friend is there. It is a shared joy, a sure trust.

Merry Christmas from Naples — 1983!

"All hail, KING JESUS! All hail, EMMANUEL: King of kings, Lord of lords, Bright Morning Star!"

This song of adoration rings from our church all year long in anticipation of HIS soon return! "Let ev'ry heart prepare HIM room, and heav'n and nature sing, and heav'n and nature sing!"

Nature is indeed exultant around me. Pink hibiscus blossoms wave in the breeze over my head, attracting hummingbirds. Yellow allamandas crown the chain fence, which tries unsuccessfully to hide from me the frisky mullet splashing back into the canal after joyous leaps of freedom through the air. Palm trees leaning against the sky take my thoughts back to the Judean hills where shepherds still graze their flocks. Could some of them, too, be expecting the return of MESSIAH? A brief toe-dip into the pool evokes a hearty welcome to the warm December sun. A colorful butterfly hopping and skipping past reminds me of rapidly fleeting years!

Obeying the injunction to be fruitful and multiply, we welcomed Lloyd Christian Regas into the clan in April in Jacksonville, and six weeks later Zachary Eugene Modlin in Hickory, North Carolina. This doubled our male progeny to four, along with our nine girls. All twenty-six of us chose to share a merry Thanksgiving together in Newnan this year, in lieu of a Merry Christmas gathering.

I find I am occupied full-time for Jesus, excited at what He is doing in the world today. Jim hardly knows what to expect with me these days! (Isn't life supposed to embrace some mystery?) I'm currently facing ten final exams for the first trimester of Word of Faith Leadership and Bible Institute, which I attend via closed circuit TV from 8:30 AM to 12:30 PM every weekday. We are also momentarily expecting the phones to start ringing in our new 700 Club Counseling Center. As Co-Director, my main task is to train our phone counselors according to the guidelines of the Christian Broadcasting Network.

I pray that life is just as exciting and fulfilling for you all, and that abundant blessings overtake each of you in 1984!

Mary and Jim O'Callaghan and Skipper, too

America Through Christian Eyes — 1984

It is superfluous to say that 1984 is a critical election year in America. Ungodly forces are making an all-out effort on behalf of the lusts of the flesh and the deceitfulness of riches multiplied by pornography, sodomy, abortion, adultery, drugs, etc. Self-governing democracy is once again given the opportunity to choose a lifestyle according to the dictates of God's Word or according to the dictates of man's heart. God gives us that freedom. God told Samuel when Israel wanted a king that they were not rejecting Samuel's leadership over them, but they were rejecting God Himself. God allows us to make choices for evil or for good, but not without warning us of the consequences of our choices.

Though it has been plainly told him, man has not chosen to believe the fact that he inhabits two very real worlds, one seen and one unseen, one natural and one supernatural, or spiritual. Sociologists tell us that every people group has worshipped someone or something. Just as hunger and thirst were built into man to lead him to eat and drink in order to sustain his physical body, so hunger and thirst have been built into the inner man to draw him into worship, thus to sustain the hidden man of the heart.

The works of Satan, who was described by Jesus as the thief who comes to steal, kill and destroy, are manifest all around us, but many Christians as well as nonbelievers deny the truth in God's Word concerning this fallen angelic enemy. They have not understood the necessity of burying in baptism the old nature that has been tainted with death as inherited from Adam and being resurrected with Jesus unto eternal life, born again spiritually from above! (Romans 6:4). Even when he is born again, the lust of the flesh, the lust of the eyes and the pride of life constantly battle against the hungering and thirsting within the renewed inner man to worship and yield to his God. Satan tries to pervert these spiritual longings into worship of "self" or some manmade god, thus denying the Creator God.

Jesus offered Himself as the Bread of Life, requiring that we eat of Him if we would gain the Kingdom of God. We know that there are some nice soft white, palatable breads today, with additives and preservatives to guarantee long shelf life. The only problem is that they have been stripped of the life that could sustain a body. In the same way, God's Word may look and feel and taste like that tempting soft

The Government Shall Be Upon Whose Shoulder?

white bread, but when we question, along with Satan, *"Hath God said...?"* and supply our own answers, then we have stripped our Bread of its life-giving nutrients. We assure our Bibles a long life on some shelf when we agree with Satan rather than with Jesus, *"It is written..."* Only God would list the main ingredients of His Bread of Life: a cross and self-denial! The Bread of Life may not look so attractive; there is something repulsive about taking up a cross and denying self. Tribulations and persecutions are not exactly our happy daily choices. It may be harder to chew and swallow than the lifeless variety, but Jesus is in it with us, and He is the life! He is our strength and peace and joy! Taste and see!

The Earth is the Lord's and the fullness thereof. Dominion over it was given to man, not to angels. When Adam surrendered it to the illegal invader, Satan, a man who would not yield to the usurper was necessary to redeem the Earth and snatch mankind from death. Jesus came as that last Adam — no other was needed! The sacrifice was perfect and the way into God's Presence was opened for all who would accept it! It is in Christ that we have the victory over sin and death! But the dominion that Jesus bought back for us with His divine blood will be ours only if we exercise it. All authority has been given to Jesus in heaven and on Earth (Matthew 28:18), but Satan lies to us that he still has dominion over us. Satan has no authority, but he has not yet been stripped of all his power. God is still using him! As the darkness grows darker, God's glory shines ever brighter.

If we are the Body of Christ with Jesus the head, and the government is on His shoulder, then we stand in a governing position. Each person is necessary to supply his function for victory. There are soldiers on the front lines undergirded by many who are on their knees. The generals take charge and plan the strategies. Many are called to furnish the supplies, while others transport the supplies where needed. And very important are those who set themselves apart to hear from the Commander in Chief, the Lord of Hosts!

The devil has unleashed his hordes, so there can be no letup of defenses. Christians must aggressively move forward to possess the land of the spirit realm, if not of the natural. The conflagrations in the world openly manifest the desperate battles in the unseen world of the spirit. Christ's enemies must be put under His heels, establishing the victory He won at the cross almost two thousand years ago. Wars will rage upon the Earth until the Prince of Peace returns! All other peace is simply a transient illusion!

Mary M. O'Callaghan

Voting is a privilege. Choice is a privilege. Freedom is a privilege. Choice is freedom. With privilege comes responsibility. Jesus urges us not to be deceived in these last days. *"This gospel of the Kingdom will be preached in all the world as a witness to all the nations, and then the end will come"* (Matthew 24:14, NKJV). Will we see that it is done? Will we hasten His coming? Will we guard our freedom diligently enough to complete the job while we are still free?

"The grass withers, the flower fades,
But the word of our God stands forever" (Isaiah 40:8, NKJV).

1984 Greetings
from Mary and Jim O'Callaghan

"His name shall be called Wonderful, Counselor, The Mighty God, The Everlasting Father, The Prince of Peace!" (Isaiah 9:6).

"Behold, a virgin shall conceive, and bear a Son, and shall call His name Immanuel (God with Us)" (Isaiah 7:14).

"Good tidings of great joy ... shall be to all people. For unto you is born this day in the city of David a Saviour, which is Christ the Lord" (Luke 2:10,11).

And His Name Is Jesus, the Messiah

The little tree we planted twelve years ago to shade our patio corner now stretches out leafy arms high in the sky. Our scruffy little Norfolk Island pine in the front now towers majestically thirty feet into the heavens. The once head-high coconut palms now drop their clustered fruit from a height of two stories. We, too, reach upwards with the years. I keep reminding Jim that our youth is renewed like the eagle's! I grab my schoolbooks daily and dash out for classes, while Jim settles down to his coffee, paper, TV and Skipper. This is my second year via satellite of Word of Faith Leadership and Bible Institute from Dallas. Jim shakes his head in amazement, but encourages me.

The highlight of the year for the O'Callaghan clan was a week in the North Carolina mountains with five of our children's families ensconced in three houses. Unfortunately, our son Jimbo's family had prior commitments. We missed Atlanta, but are hoping to pop in this holiday season to sing carols with our thirteen grandchildren. My wanderings did get me to Atlanta for a spring conference of Pat Carver International Ministries. June found me in St. Louis for my third End-Time Handmaidens World Convention, with a focus on Israel. Then on October 9, I joined End-Time Handmaidens for my third pilgrimage to Israel, enjoying a day of sight-seeing in Athens while en route. Getting better acquainted with my roommate for those exciting sixteen days, we discovered we were both graduates of

Mary M. O'Callaghan

Randolph-Macon Woman's College in Lynchburg, Virginia! I'm older, but we love many of the same people. After a glorious, weeklong celebration of the Feast of Tabernacles, sponsored by the International Christian Embassy, Jerusalem, we moved to the Intercontinental Hotel on the Mount of Olives for our own End-Time Handmaidens Convention. We visited a three-year-old Jewish Christian settlement atop a mountain, toured the ruins of Ahab and Jezebel's palace at Sebaste, Samaria, overlooking the world (it seemed), and went north as far as the "Good Fence" at the border of Lebanon. We went east on the Golan Heights to the border of Syria guarded by U.N. troops, before returning to Tiberias on the Sea of Galilee. The most dangerous thing about going to Israel is that you find your roots and there is a persistent tugging on your heart to go back!

Our friends Helen Blair and Virginia Edgington have moved from Naples. Some dear friends have taken up a heavenly abode, as has my sister's husband, Dick Kendrick. We miss them, but are thankful that the birth of Jesus has given purpose, comfort and everlasting joy to all who claim Him as their own. May He be yours, too!

Healing Scriptures in Behalf of Zachary Modlin

February 11, 1985

Thank you for joining us in prayer for Zachary Modlin, twenty-month-old son of Laurie and Gene Modlin, and grandson of Jim and Mary O'Callaghan, diagnosed with hepatoblastoma, cancer originating in the liver. We are putting on the armor of God according to Ephesians 6:10-18 and are taking dominion over all the power of the enemy. *"Behold, I give you the authority to trample on serpents and scorpions, and over all the power of the enemy, and nothing shall by any means hurt you"* (Luke 10:19, NKJV). We will be praying according to the Word of God, *"and the prayer of faith shall save the sick"* (James 5:15).

I will hasten my word to perform it (Jeremiah 1:12).

So shall My word be that goeth forth out of My mouth: it shall not return unto Me void, but it shall accomplish that which I please, and it shall prosper in the thing whereto I sent it (Isaiah 55:11).

...the Scripture cannot be broken (John 10:35).

Surely He hath borne our griefs [translated "grief" only twice, but "sickness," "disease," etc., twenty-two times, NASB], and carried our sorrows: yet we did esteem Him stricken, smitten of God, and afflicted. But He was wounded for our transgressions, He was bruised for our iniquities: the chastisement of our peace was upon Him; and with His stripes we are healed (Isaiah 53:4,5).

...and He cast out the spirits with His word, and healed all that were sick: that it might be fulfilled which was spoken by Isaiah the prophet, saying, Himself took our infirmities, and bare our sicknesses (Matthew 8:16,17).

Who His own self bare our sins in His own body on the tree, that we, being dead to sins, should live unto righteousness: by whose stripes ye were healed (1 Peter 2:24).

Mary M. O'Callaghan

God is not a man, that He should lie. (Numbers 23:19).

Every good gift and every perfect gift is from above, and cometh down from the Father of lights, with whom is no variableness, neither shadow of turning (James 1:17).

Jesus Christ the same yesterday, and today, and for ever (Hebrews 13:8).

For this purpose the Son of God was manifested, that He might destroy the works of the devil (1 John 3:8).

How God anointed Jesus of Nazareth with the Holy Ghost and with power: who went about doing good, and healing all that were oppressed of the devil; for God was with Him (Acts 10:38).

Put Me in remembrance: let us plead together, declare thou, that thou mayest be justified (Isaiah 43:26).

And the prayer of faith shall save the sick, and the Lord shall raise him up; and if he have committed sins, they shall be forgiven him. Confess your faults one to another, that ye may be healed. The effectual fervent prayer of a righteous man availeth much (James 5:15,16).

For He hath made Him to be sin for us, who knew no sin; that we might be made the righteousness of God in Him (2 Corinthians 5:21).

I am the LORD [Jehovah — covenant keeper, grace giver, who dwells among His people] that healeth thee (Exodus 15:26). (God originated healing and it is His expressed will to heal.)

And ye shall serve the LORD your God, and He shall bless thy bread, and thy water; and I will take sickness away from the midst of thee (Exodus 23:25).

The Government Shall Be Upon Whose Shoulder?

The thief cometh not, but for to steal, and to kill, and to destroy: I am come that they might have life, and that they might have it more abundantly (John 10:10).

Submit yourselves therefore to God. Resist the devil, and he will flee from you (James 4:7).

But if the Spirit of Him that raised up Jesus from the dead dwell in you, He that raised up Christ from the dead shall also quicken your mortal bodies by His Spirit that dwelleth in you (Romans 8:11).

Greater is He that is in you, than he that is in the world (1 John 4:4).

Beloved, I wish above all things that thou mayest prosper and be in health, even as thy soul prospereth (3 John 2).

…and great multitudes followed Him, and He healed them all (Matthew 12:15).

Who forgiveth all thine iniquities; who healeth all thy diseases; who redeemeth thy life from destruction; who crowneth thee with loving-kindness and tender mercies (Psalm 103:3,4).

Then they cry unto the LORD in their trouble, and He saveth them out of their distresses. He sent His word, and healed them, and delivered them from their destructions (Psalm 107:19,20).

Psalm 91. (Personalize all, especially verses 5-6, 9-10, 14-16.)

And these signs shall follow them that believe; in My name shall they cast out devils; they shall speak with new tongues; they shall take up [away] serpents; and if they drink any deadly thing, it shall not hurt them; they shall lay hands on the sick, and they shall recover (Mark 16:17-18).

Mary M. O'Callaghan

There came also a multitude ... bringing sick folks, and them which were vexed with unclean spirits: and they were healed every one (Acts 5:16).

But without faith it is impossible to please Him: for he that cometh to God must believe that He is, and that He is a rewarder of them that diligently seek Him (Hebrews 11:6).

Jesus said unto him, If thou canst believe, all things are possible to him that believeth (Mark 9:23).

Sanctify them through Thy truth: Thy word is truth (John 17:17).

Have faith in God. For verily I say unto you, that whosoever shall say unto this mountain, Be thou removed, and be thou cast into the sea; and shall not doubt in his heart, but shall believe that those things which he saith shall come to pass; he shall have whatsoever he saith. Therefore I say unto you, what things soever ye desire, when ye pray, believe that ye receive them, and ye shall have them. And when ye stand praying, forgive. (Mark 11:22-25).

No weapon that is formed against thee shall prosper; and every tongue that shall rise against thee in judgment thou shalt condemn. This is the heritage of the servants of the LORD, and their righteousness is of Me, saith the LORD (Isaiah 54:17).

For ever, O LORD, Thy word is settled in heaven (Psalm 119:89).

My son, attend to my words; incline thine ear unto my sayings. Let them not depart from thine eyes; keep them in the midst of thine heart. For they are life unto those that find them, and health to all their flesh (Proverbs 4:20-22).

And this is the confidence [boldness] that we have in Him, that if we ask any thing according to His will, He heareth us: and if we know that He hear us, whatsoever we ask, we know that we have the petitions that we desired of Him (1 John 5:14,15).

The Government Shall Be Upon Whose Shoulder?

Father, in the name of Jesus, I thank You that Zachary shall not die but shall live and declare Your works. And though this is impossible with men, it is not with You, for all things are possible with You. I will not weaken in faith and consider Zachary's body; no unbelief or distrust will make me waver or doubtingly question concerning Your promise. I am strong and empowered by faith as I give praise and glory to You, for I am assured that You are able and mighty to keep Your word and to do what You have promised. I thank You that it is done, in Jesus' name. Amen, so be it!

From Zachary's Parents

Hickory, North Carolina
March 12, 1985

Dear Friends,

    As many of you may know at this point, Zachary went to be with the Lord on March 2. While we certainly continue to miss him tremendously, many things have lightened our sorrow.

    Though we do not pretend that this is the answer to prayer we were hoping for, it is nonetheless true that Zachary is now totally, perfectly, eternally healed and whole. I think it is true that parents would rather release their child, God's gift to them, back to God's loving hands than to see him/her suffer for a prolonged time. We were grateful at the time of diagnosis, and still are, that Zachary's sickness was such that he either had to be totally healed quickly or go to the Father.

    Even during his sickness, there were medical miracles that several people reminded us of. Zachary never reached an intolerable pain level, and he rarely complained. Whereas most cancer patients at advanced stages can exist only on strong painkillers and nonetheless suffer, he needed only Tylenol III in limited quantities. We were able to keep him at home with us and keep him fairly comfortable. We are grateful for that time and that miracle.

    Certainly there are questions, and each of us is going to have to come to manageable answers for himself — knowing all the while we see only dimly now and can't have full understanding. We are able to rest ourselves in one of the most difficult areas — we KNOW we did the best we knew scripturally and medically, and in that there is no reproach. We did, indeed, with many others fight the good fight of faith and Zachary did receive the prize of the upward call of God in Christ Jesus. Though we longed for a physical healing and still fervently believe that it is God's expressed will to pray for such, we rest, again KNOWING our God is loving, compassionate and just — to Zachary as well as us. That lessens the hurt to a large extent. While there are always mysteries, God's character remains constant; and when questions come, we must fall back on Who He is.

The Government Shall Be Upon Whose Shoulder?

Our friends and family have ministered to us in such a way that many have seen the need to reevaluate their lives, both personally and within the Church. It has been the love of Christ in ACTION through the Body of Christ. We know, too, that we've had more prayers for us by all of you than we can imagine. How can we thank you? Just know your prayers are being answered. It is a painful process, but we do have the victory. We have said all along that God would receive ALL the victory through this, and we stick by it.

"Death is swallowed up in victory. O death, where is your victory? O death, where is your sting? ... Thanks be to God, who gives us the victory through our Lord Jesus Christ" (1 Corinthians 15:54-57, NKJV).

The ultimate victory is that through the whole situation and through the service especially, all present learned of our living Hope, and I know many were challenged to accept Him for themselves.

As for us here and now, we're down in Naples, Florida, visiting with my parents and some family for a couple of weeks. If you've written, these letters will overlap. We love you all and have learned in a new way the importance of friends who stand by you.

We appreciate your continued prayers for us, especially as we go back home and resume life there.

In Jesus' love and hope,
Laurie and Gene

Happy Holy Days,
The O'Callaghans — 1985

How we rejoice to celebrate the birth of our Lord Jesus, Emmanuel, God With Us, who came to reconcile us unto Himself! Because He lives we know our little Zachary lives and even now rejoices with the angelic heavenly host as we on Earth prepare for the soon return of Jesus and our reunion together! God's promises are so precious, and having received the earnest of our inheritance, the baptism in the Holy Spirit, we look forward to the full inheritance as heirs together with Christ. Hallelujah!

This has been a year of changes for our portion of the clan. In June, Marky married Ron Underwood, a twenty-year Delta pilot, now with a consolidated family of six children — in her Mom's footsteps! The children gave them to each other at the wedding. Sheri is a twenty-one-year-old senior at Auburn. Ronnie is a high school senior, as is Lisa, Marky's oldest. Michael is thirteen, Amy is twelve and Benjie is almost eleven. It is a good thing she wasn't able to sell her big house! Michael lives with his mother in Pennsylvania; the rest live with Marky and Ron. George MacNabb has remarried and lives in Newnan, still in the family with Cindy married to his brother Bill.

We all shared deeply in Laurie and Gene's grief after liver cancer claimed our precious little Zachary, twenty-one months old. God was faithful with some miracles along the way, and they are expecting their arms to be filled once again by year's end. They have been upheld by many wonderful friends in Hickory, North Carolina, six or seven of whom are sharing in the population explosion with them. Gene and his partner are taking over an in-town dental practice as well as their other office. He and Laurie have bought a house and hope to be in their own nest before Christmas and baby-day. Jim and I have made no special plans, but I am on call for nursery duty when needed.

It pleases us that our six children find the ways and means to get together, in Birmingham with the Barneses (Karen), in Atlanta with the MacNabbs (Cindy) or the O'Callaghans (Jimbo), in Newnan at the MacNabb-Underwood "Motel" (Marky, Ron, Sheri, Ronnie and Lisa all have cars), in Hickory with the Modlins (Laurie), in Jacksonville with the Regas fivesome (Wendy turns thirty December 13, and here I am only thirty-nine!), and best of all, in Naples with us. Wendy

The Government Shall Be Upon Whose Shoulder?

and her family spent Thanksgiving week with us, building sand castles and frolicking at the beach. (I went into the Gulf too, and it was delicious.) Chris tried the championship course at the new condominium Jim invested in. The Thanksgiving buffet at the Royal Poinciana, complete with ice sculptures, is breathtakingly beautiful and delicious, making us aware of how blessed and thankful we really are! Marky used her pass to fly down overnight to laze on the beach with us, declaring the "Delta-wife" way is fun.

I finished my two years at Word of Faith Leadership and Bible Institute (via satellite), and I am still affiliated with Pat Carver Ministries in Atlanta. I still minister at the jail on Sunday nights with two friends. Jim always surprises me when I go out of town. He took a real estate course and is now taking an active role with the Holdridge Company a few blocks from home.

Our love for each of you goes with this annual greeting, and our prayers for the very best for you and yours and for our nation in 1986!

1986 Christmas Greetings — The O'Callaghans

JOY to the world! Most of the world doesn't know that JOY'S name is Jesus! Most of the world doesn't know that Jesus is the Son of the living God, Creator of all that is, and that He is the same yesterday, today and forever. Most of the world doesn't know that in the beginning He already was, the very Word, the outshining expression of the God who changes not, who is unconditional Love, full of grace and mercy. Because we were created to worship Him, the entire world has sought Him, even though they might not have known who, or what, or where He is. The one whom Jesus called the "prince of this world" has blinded eyes, offering deceiving substitutes for the real JOY who became flesh and dwelt among us. Those of us who know Him and live in Him, and He in us, are commissioned to tell what Christmas is all about — JOY to the world!

What a special blessing last Christmas Eve in Hickory when grandchild fourteen arrived, Thaddeus James Modlin. A Christmas call confirmed that Laurie and daddy Gene, who determined not to spend all of Christmas Day in the hospital, were indeed nestled by a cozy fire in their very own "new" house with little Thad in their arms. God is so good!

Our unique (for us) 1986 event was a fourth of July "C.A. Mees Family Reunion" at my brother Don's in Lawrenceville, Georgia, sixty-two strong. The O'Callaghan branch accounted for twenty-eight plus Skipper. Jim and I had offered prizes for the best "memoirs" essay in four age categories. We called it a draw, and Jim gave all thirty of them, school age and under, commemorative Statue of Liberty silver dollars. I spent the rest of the summer digging up and duplicating old pictures and news clippings of our illustrious forebears, collating twenty-five "Family Albums" with said "memoirs."

Jim comes home whistling every day from the real estate office, not that he is selling that much, but he enjoys being a "useful flunky," as he puts it. His main exercise these days consists of strolling on the pier, checking out the fishing boats at the city dock and walking the dog down the street several times a day, plus, of course, a lot of armchair quarterbacking. I do keep reminding him our youth is renewed like the eagle's. He is thrilled to at last have progeny at Georgia Tech! Granddaughter Lisa MacNabb, with Star Student scholarships

The Government Shall Be Upon Whose Shoulder?

tucked under her arm, donned a rat cap in September. (Do they still do that?)

The world situation prompts me to spend most of my time in Bible study and intercession, with two or three weekly meetings in our house, plus jail ministry on Sunday nights. I'm still associated with Pat Carver Ministries and End-Time Handmaidens, and find myself back on the local Women's Aglow board (an international charismatic organization). Signs of the times, current prophecies and biblical prophecies all point to a soon return of Jesus (1 Thessalonians 3:13, 1 Timothy 6:14, Titus 2:13). Jesus says, in parable form, that the virgins with oil who are prepared and watching will go forth to meet the Bridegroom (Matthew 25:1-13). These are most exciting days! As surely as He entered this Earth as a babe, and ascended to a heavenly throne, He'll return just as He has said! (Revelation 22:7, 12, 13, 16, 20).

May we close with the final blessing and verse in His Holy Word, "The grace of our Lord Jesus Christ be with you all. Amen" (Revelation 22:21) and amen!

O'Callaghan Merry Christmas — 1987

"HARK! THE HERALD ANGELS SING, 'GLORY TO THE NEW-BORN KING.'" *Angel* literally means "messenger," and we too herald the King of kings, to the praise of His glory, as we spread the message of His redeeming love. According to the Apostle Paul, our whole purpose is to be *"to the praise of His glory"* (Ephesians 1:12).

1987 has been a Jubilee year for us. I returned to Atlanta to celebrate my fiftieth North Fulton High School reunion in April and got the prize for the most grandchildren. In retrospect, I advocate at least twenty-five-year reunions, because after fifty years the standard greeting becomes, "And who are you?" Then early in November we returned for the Georgia Tech Homecoming celebration of Jim's fiftieth reunion. They stop counting after fifty years and induct them all into the "Old Golds' Club." It was great to be with old buddies, if only briefly, and enjoy the game and the ever-changing Atlanta skyline from the exclusive height of the President's Box. Jim's compliment was indicative of the age bracket we now grace, "Honey, you were the best preserved gal there." (No doubt it was indicative of dimming eyesight as well, since that Depression-educated, World War II Veteran group looked pretty good!)

The passing years have also effected another change in our lives. Since Jim hasn't golfed in a couple years, we closed our membership in the Royal Poinciana Golf Club and joined the new Collier Athletic Club. Once again I regularly don my leotard (or bathing suit), and ten minutes from our door I'm huffing and puffing to low-impact aerobics with the cute young instructors who are helping preserve the geriatric generation. Jim has limited his athletic endeavors to one game of "pool" with our son-in-law Chris Regas when Wendy and family joined us from Jacksonville for Thanksgiving to relax in the sun and splash in the Gulf.

More and more my life is involved in that "praise of His glory." I still hold credentials with Pat Carver Ministries and have been a jack-of-all-trades in our Naples Women's Aglow Fellowship. Besides the regular Bible study in our home and in the jail, I've been to some exciting conventions and seminars. How ironic that we can't mention God in our schools but can minister His grace in jails and prisons after lives have been shattered without Him! I made my fourth pilgrimage to Israel with the End-Time Handmaidens to gloriously celebrate the Feast of Tabernacles

The Government Shall Be Upon Whose Shoulder?

with the International Christian Embassy, Jerusalem. (See Zechariah 14:16 ff.) We began with our first End-Time Handmaidens French Convention in Paris before heading for our twelfth Jerusalem Convention.

God continues to "fruitfully bless" the O'Callaghans. In May, Wendy will increase the Regas family with a fourth child, and Laurie and Gene Modlin will present Thad with a little sibling (grandchildren numbers fifteen and sixteen). That doesn't even include Ron's additions to Marky's family, increasing the total to nineteen. The rest of the clan is status quo, and a year older.

Jim continues to go to the real estate office daily, reads extensively, works the crossword puzzles; and armchair quarterbacks. We'll head to Atlanta where the clan will gather once again to celebrate Messiah's birth. And in His name we wish each and every one of you LOVE and JOY and PEACE now and throughout 1988!

Joyous Christmas
From Jacksonville — 1988

Merry Christmas! This is a new era for Jim, Skipper and me as we settle into our new "love nest." We leave the mullet splashing in our Naples canal, the yellow allamanda blossoms that share the view toward the bay, the little doves that timidly gather seeds scattered by the cardinals and mockingbirds, the mango trees that lusciously supply, along with the limes, key limes and avocados, the powdery white beach with the daily cache of shells that so gloriously frames the incomparable Naples sunsets, not to mention the wonderful friends with whom we have been blessed for over seventeen years! But we are not entirely uprooted, for we still have condos there.

We feel back in the mainstream of life here ten minutes from Wendy's family and some three-hundred-plus miles closer to the other five children. According to their instructions, we now have an even larger house in expectation of more frequent visits and have gained a hot tub adjoining the pool. We are on a hill and the backyard is wooded, all reminiscent of Atlanta. Unopened cartons still crowd the garage while we ponder where to put our forty-seven-year accumulation of books, tapes, rocks, shells and other important (to us only) memorabilia. We are about five minutes from the Epping Forest Yacht Club on the St. Johns River (the old DuPont estate) where Jim can continue to check out boats, fishing, etc., and I can resume some aerobics and fine dining once we finish papering, painting, hanging and assembling. We are also close to the Mayo Clinic, where Jim had checked in for tests in May. While there, Wendy's fourth child, our fifteenth grandchild, arrived, Allison Stephanie Regas, a little surprise redhead! A couple of weeks later, Laurie presented us with number sixteen, Hayes Eugene Modlin, in Hickory. See why we need a bigger house? Jim is still checking in with Mayo, and we feel we are in good hands.

In February I met Kari Bakke from Norway when I attended the End-Time Handmaidens School of Ministry in Arkansas, and she has visited us in Naples a couple times. Kari has been in the forefront of the move of the Holy Spirit in northern Europe since the early seventies, and is a "watchman" concerning the New Age movement (really old Babylon). I visited her for Christian conferences in Arendal, Norway, a quaint, hilly seaside resort town. Her son and daughter gave

The Government Shall Be Upon Whose Shoulder?

me a private tour of Oslo, including nearby ski slopes. They have both been exchange students here in America. We are hoping Kari can find a place here in Jacksonville to winter, since she loves Florida (particularly Naples). We'll work together "Under His Wings," our ministry of reconciliation according to Luke 9:1,2. Pat Carver will be our first speaker here in Jacksonville in January.

Above all, Jim and I are glad that we are in the Lord's hands, whose birth we now celebrate. Jesus is the Child that was born, the Son that was given, who shed His blood and tasted death for us all, was resurrected and will soon return from His throne on high to claim a Bride who is now preparing herself. Hallelujah! I aim to stay ready! Come, Lord Jesus!

Years fly by ever more quickly, with friends and family ever more valuable. Like shiny jewels you all decorate our precious Christmas memories. May 1989 be a year of stored-up treasures for each of you. We love and appreciate you.

Holy Holidays — 1989

JESUS is LORD! That is the most important statement that can be made, not only at this Christmas season but also from now until HIS appearing! Others may claim to be the Christ, and other people may "lord" it over your life, but rest assured, JESUS alone is LORD! HE is the CHRIST of Christmas, so celebrate this unspeakable gift from on high!

A year after moving into our little palace we still wonder where things are, which may be a sign of our age. We were extremely happy in our tropical Neapolitan paradise, but from that early morning chat when Jim said, "Maybe we should take advantage of the real estate market and sell the house," and I said, "I'm not married to Naples; where shall we move?" we hastily decided on Jacksonville, since we didn't want to leave Florida. Neither one of us has looked back with a moment of regret. Amazing! A shock to all the family and even to us! I picked the house out, sight unseen by Jim, with all the features I knew he'd like. Once I put my roots into a church, I'm "at home." Jim feels "at home" because he can drive to the corner for an Atlanta newspaper, to properly readjust his wandering blood pressure, and on Sundays drive to First Presbyterian Church in the inner city. I go to the early service at my church, New Life Christian Fellowship, to join him for the ride to town and a lunch date after that service. It is a little quieter than in the "olden days" when the eight of us would pile into the car after the service at Central Presbyterian in downtown Atlanta to head to the Club or to the Varsity at Tech for lunch. Only on two occasions did we discover that we had left a child at church.

Wendy and Chris have only four children and they have already left one at church. Is it an old family custom? We are enjoying their varied activities, particularly the adroitness of eighteen-month-old Allison to completely rule her household and two sets of grandparents. The other eleven grandchildren and their five sets of parents are more regular visitors now that we are closer to them all. Once again we spread sleeping bags all over the house as they spend the nights back and forth. The hot tub is an attractive bonus after games in the pool. To add to the fun, Marky's Amy has moved into an apartment near us with her baby Kristen Ashley, born in August. She is taking some courses to get her high school diploma.

The Government Shall Be Upon Whose Shoulder?

Jim doesn't complain, but stays home to balance his medications to balance his equilibrium. I'm doing great and took off three weeks for Egypt, Israel and Norway, with a day in Copenhagen, since Wendy was here to look in on her Dad. I went with Kari and a group from Norway (no, I don't speak Norwegian) and was delighted we were in the same hotel in Jerusalem with the End-Time Handmaidens for the Christian celebration of the Feast of Tabernacles. That's a forerunner of Zechariah 14:16, in case you are wondering. It was my fifth pilgrimage to Israel, that important little piece of land where Messiah Jesus will make His Second Advent. Those who truly study prophecy know it can't be long now, because conditions are rapidly being fulfilled. Heed the Scout motto, "Be Prepared!"

Though the hair gets grayer and thinner, and the eyes dimmer, and the bones creakier, our memories grow fonder and our love stronger as we wish each of you love, joy and peace this Christmas and throughout the next decade!

Celebrate the Christ in Christmas — 1990

'Tis the season of joy; 'tis the season of hope, for God Himself chose to enter the realm of time to bring man back to Himself to share His glory! Indeed His Peace came on Earth as a babe so that eternal Peace might dwell with men eternally! Rejoice with great joy!

Welcome God's Peace, the risen Lord Jesus, King of the Jews, Holy One of Israel, Son of David, born in Bethlehem ("House of Bread"), the city of David! He has taken all our confessed guiltiness upon Himself, enduring for us the curse of God's law that calls for obedience to the purity of His perfection. He clothes us in a robe of righteousness so we can fellowship with our Father. He bore crushing stripes that we might be healed. Nothing is lacking in the salvation He bought for us (spirit, soul and body) with His precious blood. He is coming back soon for a Bride prepared and waiting, without spot or blemish. Proclaim with the angels, "GLORY TO GOD IN THE HIGHEST, AND ON EARTH PEACE, GOOD WILL TOWARD MEN."

As we push towards our fiftieth anniversary next June, peace reigns in the O'Callaghan home, even as we agree with friends, "Old age ain't for sissies." It has been a tough year physically for Jim, but his sense of humor helps carry him through. A slight heart attack (with a twinkle, the doctor called it a "coronette," for a little "coronary"), followed by a little stroke last January, left him only slightly impaired. Poor circulation in his legs and feet has greatly limited his mobility.

We are delighted to live in Jacksonville to enjoy Wendy and Chris's family, plus more frequent visits from all our other five families. Laurie and Gene are expecting to present us with grandchild number seventeen in March. After a family of boys, they are hoping this little "Tar Heel" will don pink, for variety's sake.

After several years' absence, we did get to Atlanta for several days of Thanksgiving. Forgive us for not visiting with beloved old friends, for whom we are very thankful. Our brief time was spent surrounded by twenty-three family members who had coerced Jim into the trip, lovingly providing for all his physical comforts and desires. They were gratified to be able to reciprocate for the spoiling he had lovingly poured out on them in years past. At one time there were fifteen of us plus two cats and one dog sleeping at Cindy and Bill's house! Did I say sleeping?

The Government Shall Be Upon Whose Shoulder?

I managed one trip this year, to Austin, Texas, for a conference and seminar (three hours college credit) with YAVO Ministries (Hebrew for "He is coming"), on the Hebrew Foundations of Our Faith. Dr. Roy Blizzard, former professor at the University of Texas, was the teacher. Now surrounded by reference books, tapes, etc., I'm learning a little Hebrew, to delve deeply into what is most important to me. His name is Jesus!

Once again we rejoice to celebrate with you His coming and look forward to His soon return!

Happy New Year all 1991 long!!!

Christmas Greetings from the Modlins

Having just returned from a blessed yet sweltering Jacksonville Thanksgiving, where our hopes for a seasonal "nip" in the air went unrealized, and where our festive autumnal garb was quickly exchanged for gym shorts and T-shirts, it's hard to believe that Christmas is a mere two weeks away. I'm dreaming of a white Christmas???!

1991 has been a year of myriad changes for the Modlins, from the grand and glorious to the perhaps more mundane, that nonetheless fills the majority of our lives. First and foremost, Hillary Katherine made her way into the world and our hearts on... (I know you won't believe this, but I just had to stop and check the calendar for her birth date. I'm glad I did — I was off by two days! They'll let anyone be parents these days.) Anyway, Hillary graced us with her presence on March 22. The surprise and joy of being blessed with this precious girl stays with us, and no one is more thrilled than Thad, who was rooting for a girl all along. (Hayes, on the other hand, was hoping for boy "Connor" and recently asked if the next time God gave out a baby, could he give us baby "Connor?" Sorry, Hayes!)

After the first three months of "settle-in" time, Hillary has been the sweetest, happiest, cutest thing around. She approaches nine months with four teeth, a toe-push belly-rub crawl, big blue eyes (from where?), squeezable chipmunk cheeks, an adorable smile and a winning disposition. On to big change number two.

We now have an official school-goer in our midst. Thad donned backpack and blue jeans to join the ranks of kindergartners at our neighborhood school one block away. I am truly amazed as I see our prayers for an easy adjustment and a good year for him being answered under less than ideal classroom circumstances. We've watched him blossom into a "big" boy over the last two months as he's learned to ride his bike, walks to and from school by himself, and is learning to read in bounds. He still is very self-conscious, but growing; he's a thinker, a rule-follower (like his Mom!), private with his feelings (like his Dad!), sweet, loving, a good prayer and a *great* big brother — all the time to Hillary, and most of the time to Hayes.

Hayes, too, has had change as he started three-year-old preschool two mornings a week. He stays full of life — loves to smile and sing, kiss and hug. He really is terribly sweet and, for the most part, quite easy to get along with. He

The Government Shall Be Upon Whose Shoulder?

adores Thad, and last week asked, "When does my best friend 'T.J.' get home from school? I miss him so-o-o-o much." And he really loves Hillary, though since she doesn't play, her worth at times seems in question. His impish grin gets him out of tight places on occasion, which he knows, and that's okay.

And finally, for our last big change, we announce the addition of Modlin pet number one (if you don't count our two not-so-fortunate goldfish), MOLLIE THE CAT. She is loved by one and all with the exception of me, and I'm learning to tolerate her well enough.

On the more daily front, Gene has added to his usual work/play schedule church volleyball and a Saturday AM men's prayer/fellowship group. I've added Moms-in-Touch (a weekly prayer group for our school) and being in Thad's class as often as opportunity arises and schedule allows. I am also looking forward to a study group starting in January called "Experiencing God."

On the extended family front, we'd appreciate continued prayer for my folks. Dad's had another rough year physically, which has, of course, been difficult for them both. Like a trooper, he keeps his wit and sense of humor whenever there's a break in the discomfort. Sometimes it is not easy to see the Lord's hand clearly in such tough circumstances, but that is exactly our continued prayer.

Our holiday plans include Christmas in Lincolnton with Gene's folks and both siblings' families (his folks had to make an addition on their house to hold us all!) and then on to Atlanta for a few days with some of my siblings.

Although we haven't had a chance to see many of you this year, our love extends over the miles to you all. And our prayer this year for us all is found in a song I recently heard for the first time. It speaks of Mary and Joseph and the very real and tough decisions they had to make in yielding their hearts, and wills, to God concerning the coming of the One whose birth we now celebrate. "And in one quiet moment, a woman and man accepted the part they would have in God's plan." May we do the same this season and always!

    Merry Christmas and love,
    Gene, Laurie, Thad, Hayes and Hillary

Christmas Joy — 1991, from Mary and Jim O'Callaghan

ADVENT: Latin, *ad* = "to"; *venire* = "to come." God chose to come!

God entered our time-space continuum by means of a Son, Seed of a woman, just as He proclaimed in the Garden of Eden (Genesis 3:15). The remainder of the Bible, Old and New Testaments, is the unfolding of this declared Word of God. His name was to be Yeshua, "Saviour," for He was Emmanuel, "God With Us" (Matthew 1:21-23). In the fullness of time He was sent forth, to come to (*ad venire*) us, that we might also become sons of God and heirs of the Father with Messiah Jesus (Galatians 4:4-6). This ineffable gift of the Son, whose advent we celebrate at this season, is yours for the taking! (Romans 10:9,10). We celebrate the birth of a baby, the Son of Man, and we receive the Son of God, according to God's covenant through Abraham, Isaac and Jacob, renamed "Israel" by God. There is no other way to the Father!

On our journey to the Father, we O'Callaghans count three landmark events in 1991; two occurred on the same day, March 22. While Jim was having surgery here in Jacksonville to remove his left leg below the knee because of circulatory problems and intense chronic pain, Miss Hillary Katherine Modlin put in her appearance in Hickory. She is a petite little miss, the delight of her brothers Thad and Hayes, and a surprise change of gender for Laurie and Gene after having had three boys. This little number seventeen no doubt, but no guarantees, rounds out our roll of grandchildren blessings.

On June 14 Jim and I celebrated that golden event, our Fiftieth Wedding Anniversary! Five of our children were on hand with families, and Cindy and Bill had been here just a short time before. They sent a beautiful centerpiece to represent them. We couldn't make big plans ahead of time, as the children would have liked, because of Jim's unpredictable good and bad days. Chris's mom and dad joined us for the celebration, it being Wendy and Chris's anniversary also. Would you believe we brought in Chinese food for the big occasion? Jim joined us at the big family table, and we taped the conversation and literary presentations of each one, midst much laughter and hilarity. (O'Callaghans are not noted for their subdued stoicism, but compete loudly and long and wholeheartedly at everything!) When time came for unwrapping the big box, there was breathtaking silence. Out came a large

The Government Shall Be Upon Whose Shoulder?

handmade quilt, put together with squares made by each family member, with help from mothers for the little ones. Each square pictured something special and memorable about each one and is a most precious "family treasure."

Jim still owes me an *Anniversary Waltz*, which I'll collect in the privacy of our home when he gets comfortable with his prosthesis. He has suffered much phantom limb pain, all of which has been an education to us. He had thought that with the leg gone, the pain would be gone also. But it wasn't so. His right leg is none too good, and with all his medication he really has not been out of the house except to go to the doctor. I marvel at his patience and uncomplaining endurance, and we both know much prayer sustains us. My home and church are the center of my life, so I am happy not getting out "into the world." Our greatest blessings are family and friends, so be assured of your preciousness to us as we send our love to you this Christmas, 1991.

Second Advent = *Parousia* (Greek — "appearing")

Jesus read from Isaiah 61:1,2 in the synagogue in Nazareth, and proclaimed that the *"acceptable year of the Lord"* had arrived (Luke 4:19,21). He closed the scroll with the verse unfinished, because *"the day of vengeance of our God"* was for yet another time. Beloved, *that* day rapidly approaches, the day of a Second Advent, when Messiah Jesus will return to judge the Earth, having offered salvation already to all who would receive it. Matthew tells us the good news of the Kingdom of God will be preached in all the world and then the end will come (Matthew 24:14). Just as all prophecy was fulfilled accurately concerning the First Advent, so will it be for the Second. Beloved, don't let another day pass without being sure YOU stand as a child of God!

The Regas Family — 1991

Dear Family and Friends,

Merry Christmas and a Happy New Year from the Regas family. "We feel good; oh, we feel so good — ungh!" That was the battle cry as Meredith's (age ten) Pop Warner Football Cheerleading Team made its way to National Competition. They took first place in the city in November, on to first at Regional in Miami at Thanksgiving (where Chris and Meredith enjoyed turkey at Karen Regas's Coconut Grove cabana), and went on to capture the title of Number One Peewee Cheerleaders in the nation! Chris pointed out that surely there were no better in the rest of the world or even parts beyond, so we have a Number One Cheerleader in the Universe right under our roof!

Anastasia turned thirteen this December with a b/g (boy/girl, for the uninitiated) hayride and cookout. We are relieved to see that most of the boys' energy at this point is directed toward food fights! Meanwhile, the girls have sprouted a telephone from their right ear, and we have entered the rude but convenient realm of "call waiting." Anastasia enjoys seventh grade at Bolles, where she and four girlfriends were equipment managers for the middle school football team this fall.

Lloyd (eight) loves whatever sport is in season — basketball, for now. Chris has a real gift for coaching his (and the girls') teams, which gift I'm glad he discovered late enough in life that I am spared being a professional coach's wife! Lloyd had a big summer of All-Star baseball, then fall baseball.

Allison (three) is my constant companion. She loves school (two days), dogs, sports, books, being a boy (we remind her she can PRETEND to be an Indian boy!) and Perry Mason. Her real preference is a cartoon diet.

The last year has had some curves in the roller coaster that we would rather not have hit, but the ride is still a thrill. Last January Father Paul and Penny and family accepted a call to the Cathedral in Denver and took our hearts with them **(Author's note — their Greek Orthodox priest and very close family friends).** We indulged in a twelve-day visit with them this summer, hiking and revisiting old friends and haunts, convincing ourselves that friendships do, indeed, endure the miles. I thought getting through Easter without them meant we were well adjusted, but Christmas has been raw. Everything takes time!

The Government Shall Be Upon Whose Shoulder?

Time is one thing we continue to enjoy with parents here. Frieda and Lloyd keep up a healthy pace of work, fun, travel and spectating at grandchildren's sports events. Mom and Dad give new meaning to fortitude and courage as he fights the pain from his leg amputation last March. The Christian virtues exhibited through this ordeal are a real value lesson for us all, and we are thankful to have them so close.

As for Chris and me, we keep falling in love through this adventure called life. Chris hums along at a steady pace of work and play, while I frenetically search for organization and perfection. We've managed to carve out some unusual time together, working at our fitness club at 5:30 AM three days a week (Monday, Wednesday and Friday)! We each enjoy our own personal renewal time, Chris at men's church prayer morning and I at my Precept Bible Study. It's great! We're spending lots of time with the many new Russian immigrants we've befriended, trying to help them with jobs, etc., and receiving more in blessings than we could give.

The desire for both of us continues to be to live for Christ, and in that living to let His love pour out. It's painful to fall short so often, but as the guy in *City Slickers* learned, "There's just one thing that matters." "Forgetting what is behind and straining toward what is ahead, I press on toward the goal to win the prize for which God has called me heavenward in Christ Jesus" (Philippians 3:13-14, NIV). Our prayer at this season is that each of us may become a Bethlehem for His birth and a shining star to those searching for the stable.

Keep in touch, and let's get together in 1992!

Love,
Wendy and Chris,
Anastasia, Meredith, Lloyd and Allison

Christmas 1992, The Regas Household

Twas the month before Christmas, and all through the house
we were elbow to elbow. (No room for a mouse!)
So we're buying some land to develop, sell, and build,
and waiting for Santa our stockings to fill.
We hope for a new home in '93 or '4
to make room for "Baby five." (Yep, there's one more!)
The stockings say Anastasia (thirteen), Meredith (eleven),
    and Lloyd (nine),
Allison (four), and "Hershey" — dog. What else is in store?
Why look! Santa's early! Come share our surprise
as we peek in the stocking of baby number five!
ZOIE LEIGH
November 12, 1992
Nine pounds ten ounces
Twenty-one and three-quarter inches
May God bless you all for your friendship most dear.
Merry Christmas to all, and a Happy New Year!

    Wendy, Chris and five young Regases

Be Blessed This Christmas, 1992! — Mary and Jim O'Callaghan

A young boy in Atlanta and a little girl five years younger in Charlotte were destined to grow up and become one over fifty-one years ago. How blessed are those who, like Jim and me, have a treasure-trove of precious and sweet memories of many happy years and Christmases past!

At this season we celebrate the birth almost two thousand years ago of a babe in Bethlehem ("House of Bread"), whom the angel Gabriel announced to His mother as the Son of the Most High, naming Him Yeshua, or Jesus (Luke 1:31,32). This little Jewish boy was destined to grow up and become the Bread of Life for all mankind (John 6:33). Having accomplished His mission of reconciliation at Calvary, He left Jerusalem to go back home to His Father in Heaven (John 16:28) to prepare a place for His Bride (John 14:2,3) that He might become One (John 17:20-23) with His Chosen One, the Church, both Jews and Gentiles (Revelation 19:7).

Time is different with God than with us, so that a thousand years is as a day and a day as a thousand years (2 Peter 3:8). Eternity, where Jesus lives, is "now." Eternity was always "now" and will always be "now," for the Lord God is, was, and will always be the "I AM" (Revelation 1:8). What is Jesus doing now? He is interceding for us — for you and me! (Romans 8:34). Are you born again, to enter into His kingdom? (John 3:3-7). The Spirit and the Bride say, "Come" (Revelation 22:17). Eat of the Bread of Life and take freely of the Water of Life (John 4:14), and hunger and thirst no more! (John 6:35). Enter into His rest (Matthew 11:28,29). Jesus says, "Surely, I am coming quickly."

"Amen. Even so, come, Lord Jesus! The grace of our Lord Jesus Christ be with you all. Amen" (Revelation 22:20-21, NKJV).

On November 12, two weeks before Thanksgiving, we celebrated another birth. Miss Zoie Leigh Regas, nine pounds ten ounces, filled in Wendy and Chris's roster from "A," in Anastasia (Resurrection), to "Z," in Zoie (Life)! I'm glad that I didn't guarantee last year that Laurie's Hillary was our last grand-blessing! We welcome Zoie as Wendy's fifth and our eighteenth.

Mary M. O'Callaghan

Jim was feeling well enough to host our Thanksgiving table for twenty-four, which included the senior, junior and petite Regases, Cindy and family, and a crew from Marky's who stayed at their condo on Amelia Island (Ron had to fly a football team to California), and Laurie and gang, who bunked with us. Jim indulged in a little family bridge, and a couple of the young polar bears even plunged into the pool! We're hoping Karen and hers and Jimbo and his will join us during the Christmas vacation.

As we see the truth of God exchanged in America for the lie, and the creature worshipped and served rather than the Creator (Romans 1:25 ff), and earthquakes, famines, pestilences, wars and rumors of wars, we can look up and rejoice, for surely our redemption draws nigh! (Luke 21:8-11, 28).

Share our love, and HIS, this Christmas and throughout 1993!

Modlins' Christmas Greetings — 1992

"Twas the night before December and o'er hill and dale, not a creature was stirring, not even a quail — except for travel-weary, bleary-eyed Modlins, who were determined to celebrate their memory-making, family-bonding, "tree trimming" night. You know, the night the attic fortress is looted of its myriad boxes of Christmas treasures, which are then slowly, carefully, almost reverently unpacked to reveal their cache of hidden splendor. The unveiling is met with unmasked delight. "Hayes, look what I found! Remember when we got this?"

"T.J., I'll carry the small box of breakables."

"Mom, don't you just love all the pretty decorations?"

"I remember where these go. Don't worry, I'll put them where they belong."

It's a time unlike any other, and the excitement is contagious as my mind, too, fills with the special thoughts of times, people and places that each ornament or decoration brings to mind. And that's where you come in. (I bet you thought this story wasn't going anywhere!) Because, like those treasures, except much more so, is each of you. Even if our contacts are few or far between, they are lifelong gifts that are indeed cherished.

Well, to finish that story, we did trim the tree and decorate the house to the strains of one Christmas tape after another. And while it wasn't exactly the evening we envisioned, we each in our own way now enjoy the specialness of "Christmas" around us as we sit, study, read or play. (I should mention that Hillary's enjoyment includes hiding decorations in her purse, sneaking chocolate kisses from their dish, taking bows off of packages, and, my personal favorite, dropping a Dickens caroler into the ash bucket.)

On the daily front: Thad continues to love school. I don't know if we're in a particularly good, bad or indifferent school, and I probably won't ask as long as he enthusiastically looks forward to going each day. We'll see what second grade brings. He "played" baseball and soccer this year and is probably going to attempt basketball this month. With his desire to do everything just right before even trying it the first time and his non-aggressiveness, we're not looking to set any records but hope he has fun and enjoys being on a team. Thad also looks forward to his monthly Tiger Cubs meeting with Dad and is anticipating (albeit cautiously) becoming proficient on his Christmas rollerblades from "MomO" and Papa O'Callaghan.

Mary M. O'Callaghan

Hayes, too, likes his preschool, though he was concerned about having to work on number eight this week. He manages a grin on his face most of the time, and adores big brother, little "sis" and two cats. Yes, we added kitty Izzie to play with veteran Molly, thanks to our wonderful nieces in Atlanta.

Hillary, at twenty months, is putting short sentences together, such as "Daddy's girl," and is never without at least one "nite-nite" (her pink silk pillowcase) always full of some precious treasures (little-girl talk for her sack full of toys to sleep with). She loves to tote the cats around and is finally being discouraged from holding them by the neck.

Gene and I are doing well. Work goes on; home goes on; basketball and volleyball go on. We have added a small group gathering with twelve others from our church that continues to be a good and profitable time. Any spare time is spent with some of the very special friends we are blessed with here in Hickory — and usually involves FOOD in some fashion. Speaking of food, Checkers number two is slated to open in a month or so, with high hopes for number three to follow soon after. (Note — Checkers is a business venture with friends, a chain for drive-thru, quick-service hamburgers, etc.)

Visits with friends and families have been few, but great. We just returned from a family Thanksgiving in Jacksonville, which was wonderful, because Dad felt well enough to host the Thanksgiving table as well as compete at the bridge table. Competition runs keen in the O'Callaghan clan! How special, too, to welcome baby Zoie (Wendy and Chris's number five) into the family.

On Gene's side of the family, we were saddened to say good-bye to his grandmother and great-aunt who went home to the Lord since I last wrote. We have been blessed with the peace and comfort the family has received.

Well, I'll flatter myself by saying that all good things must come to an end, as this epistle does just that. Please know how much our visits in person and by phone have meant to us. Our prayer this year for us all is that at least one aspect of the wonder and significance of our Saviour's birth will become more real this season. God's blessings on you all in 1993!!!!!

With much love,
Laurie and Gene, Thad, Hayes and Hillary

Mary's Family Letter

April 1, 1993
Jacksonville, FL

Love, grace and peace to all our precious children, grandchildren and great-grandchildren.

These are very uncertain times in which we live and I was prompted to get up early this morning and assure you of your inheritance! I can't assure you of a material inheritance, for there are elements in our government that aim to tax it away, for they think they have better ways to spend our savings than to give it to our progeny. God can change that if we diligently pray, for it is biblical to lay up an inheritance for our children and our children's children. But the church seems to lack the will or urgency to effectually and fervently pray. Certainly the heathens aren't going to pray to our God!

The inheritance I want to assure to you no one can take away! If they take away your life, you will only get it sooner! There is truly a Heaven, from which our God reigns, and there is truly a place prepared in outer darkness for the devil and all who choose to follow him. In God's love and mercy He gives to each one of us the choice, assuring us that He looks on the heart. There are only two kingdoms: one truth and the other perverted. At this point the prince, or ruler, of this world system, so called by Jesus Himself in John 12:31, 14:30 and 16:11, has already been judged and found guilty. He will very soon start serving his sentence, to be locked up for a thousand years when he can no longer deceive the people on Earth. Then after a brief time of freedom he will be cast into outer darkness, his place of perpetual destiny, along with those choosing him. It is all in The Book, God's Will and Testament. His first Will was for His family according to His union with Abraham, Isaac and Jacob. He declared Himself a husband unto His Chosen People Israel, on whom He turned His back briefly because of their unrighteousness. But He never divorced her. Now He is gathering her back unto Himself. From this union with Israel, God begat a Son by the Holy Spirit to inherit the throne and rule not only Heaven, but Earth also. God had enough love to share with many children and so He offered adoption to any who would like to join His family established on Earth. He excluded no one who

Mary M. O'Callaghan

was willing to come by faith. From this family He is calling a Bride for His Son, who is even now preparing the wedding chamber!

God wrote a second, or New Testament, or Will, to include His entire natural and engrafted family. When His only begotten Son died on the tree, this New Will became effective, and all promises therein are waiting to be claimed by all the legal heirs! Each one of you is a child of that kingdom, the Kingdom of God, by virtue of being born again, or from above, into it. You have each been dedicated to Almighty Creator God, and your inheritance is laid up for you in Heaven. You can claim it or leave it. You can even enhance it by investing your goods and your life in the Kingdom. God is a good Father who uses a system of multiplying rather than adding. I pray for each of you to receive the Spirit of God, the Spirit of Wisdom and Understanding, the Spirit of Counsel and Might, the Spirit of Knowledge and of the Fear of the Lord, according to Isaiah 11:2. THAT is your inheritance! You need no more!

Be blessed with every spiritual blessing!

"MomO" or Mother

Merry Christmas '93, from the Modlins

It's time to loose the chains of torpidity and radically change this outmoded, old-fashioned, random excuse for a data-setting, greeting-bearing, mind-expanding holiday communiqué — NOT! (Translation: Our Christmas newsletter will go on as usual.)

Ever feel caught in a language warp? What was once "cool" is now "hot"; "neat" is "awesome"; and "good" has become "bad." Language evolves, and you have to stay current or risk miscommunication. That can be especially true when speaking of Christmas. For many, the language of Christmas is comprised primarily of words such as "hurry, hurry, hurry"; "buy more gifts"; "I want..."; "I'm too busy"; and the familiar battle cry, "Charge it!" But we'd like our Christmas language to be neither that nor merely an empty seasonal greeting. We'd like to reflect the greatness of God's gift in Jesus, who can bring love, life, joy and peace to a world desperately lacking in those qualities. Our language also seeks to express appreciation for our most treasured blessings. Just as dressing and cranberry sauce are the perfect companions to a sumptuous turkey dinner, so our Christmas is wonderfully enhanced by the priceless "side dishes" of steadfast family and deeply involved friends. In an age where clear communication skills cannot be overstressed, it's our family's goal to become increasingly *unilingual!*

Speaking of family (Whew! I wondered how we'd make that transition), we are alive and thriving here in Hickory. Thad balances his time between school (he loves second grade) sports, Cub Scouts and numerous friends. Hayes is an eager kindergartner, always ready with a quick smile and a kind word. Both boys are serious about their faith and are becoming diligent prayers on behalf of family, friends and missionaries.

Hillary is a dynamo two and one-half years old. She orchestrates elaborate tea parties for her babies, rides her "bike," cuts and colors until we are paperless, and truly believes she can do anything and everything "all by myself."

As wonderful as it is to watch each child's individual growth, our greatest joy has been to see them having increased interactions. Thad and Hayes have really grown in their ability and desire to play together and enjoy each other. Hayes unashamedly names T.J. as his best friend, and Thad for his part is adamant that they share a room.

Mary M. O'Callaghan

Both the guys adore Hillary and will pretty much do anything to please her. She, of course, is aware of her power and often wields it to their detriment. But then there are the infrequent but cherished moments of a three-way hug or a shared quiet hour watching Barney or Sesame Street side by side.

As for Gene and me, we're still enjoying being challenged spiritually by our small group at church and our close friends of many years, and physically by volleyball, tennis, basketball and skiing (??). That leaves mentally, but I think that aspect got lost somewhere in the midst of kids. Gene is currently on the Building Steering Committee at church, which is in high gear right now as we're actively pursuing growth options. I still volunteer at school when possible, pray with a Moms-in-Touch group, and do payroll for Checkers (store number three coming next month). I had the naive thought that with only one child at home and no preschool schedule that life this year would be full of free time. HA!!!

The biggest outward change for us comes on Gene's work front. After ten years together, his work partner, who graduated in dentistry from the University of North Carolina with Gene, has left dentistry for law school, so Gene is planning to move out on his own. He'll lease new office space as soon as it's feasible. We're excited about that, as well as other positive work changes that have occurred during the year.

I'm delighted to report "relative" good health on both sides of the family. Once again we were thrilled to have Papa (my dad) feel well enough to bless our Thanksgiving gathering in Jacksonville. We missed the Lincolnton crew but will share festivities with all of Gene's family at Christmas.

As it is very late, we'll aptly close with...

"A MERRY CHRISTMAS TO ALL AND TO ALL A GOOD NIGHT."

Know that we are grateful for each one of you who are reading this, and for the role you've had in our lives. We pray that our hearts will be gripped afresh with the true language of Christmas.

With love,
Gene, Laurie, Thad, Hayes and Hillary

O'Callaghan Greetings for Jesus' Birthday, 1993

Thanksgiving is not over! It is our heart's preparation for the greatest GIFT ever given to mankind! God had pronounced His creation "good," but desired one in His own image and likeness to walk with Him and rule over His creation. From the elements of the earth God formed this highest of His creation, and into the lifeless nostrils God breathed His very Spirit (breath or wind). The man's heart started beating and blood started flowing, and man became a living soul! His blood was uniquely different from that of all others of God's creatures, whose life's blood was derived from God's spoken Word of command. God had a face-to-face encounter with Adam, instilling in him His very Spirit. Man was a spirit being, housed in a body of flesh, that he might fellowship with his Creator God, who is Spirit! By definition a "fellow" is one of the same class or rank; equal. God was delighted with His creation, and now pronounced it "VERY good!"

God's very essence is LOVE. Since LOVE requires an object to express itself, God fulfilled His own heart's desire for fellowship through this "man" made in His image and His likeness. Though God had pronounced creation "very good" it was "not good" for man to be alone. With compassionate love, God took a small portion out of Adam to make a helper for whom the man, in like manner, could pour forth his love! The Hebrew word for "blood" is *dam*. The initial letter for God, *Elohim*, corresponds to our "A." This creature He named *A-Dam*, "God's Blood." Adam, or man, was supposed to live forever, for the Father's blood within him was pure. God warned him that if he disobeyed the one command, not to eat of the tree of the knowledge of good and evil, "dying he would die" (literal Hebrew). This first Adam disobeyed and put himself under God's curse. Now, with blood tainted by the sting of sin, Adam was subject to death. The life of the flesh is in the blood. All of Adam's descendants have inherited tainted blood, leaving them subject to death.

With this contingency foreseen before the foundation of the world, God the Word agreed to become flesh in the fullness of time, to dwell as a Man among men. He was conceived by the Holy Spirit, Son of His Father with God's breath or Spirit, and pure divine blood. Though He was sinless, He tasted death for every man, was buried and rose again because death had no hold on Him. He was

Mary M. O'Callaghan

the firstborn of a new creation. He was the second Man, the last A-Dam (1 Corinthians 15:45-49). Jesus, the Word made flesh, said you must be born again (or from above) to share eternal life with Him. And He poured out His untainted, incorruptible, living blood that we might partake of it, to become new creatures in His new creation! His blood avails for us today because there is no sin or death in it to contaminate it! Jesus called Himself the "Son of Man." He was so in love with mankind. He sacrificed Himself for a Bride. We had no choice in our natural birth from the first Adam, but if we want to identify with Jesus, the second Man, the last A-Dam, we can make a decision in our heart and confess with our mouth that Jesus is our Lord and Saviour! It is our choice! We can come to the Heavenly Father only through the blood of Jesus!

What a strange Christmas letter, you say. But this is the essence of Christmas! God left the heavenly glory to come to Earth as a babe. He grew as a man, and is today a Man seated at the right hand of the Father, calling you to accept His gift of eternal life in glory! Fantastically awesome!!! Will you do it? Tell Him so! Jim and I have. Jesus is coming soon, and we are looking up expectantly!

MERRY CHRISTMAS and HAPPY ETERNITY!

A Soul's Prayer

Sandy MacNabb
February 26, 1994

Look into my eyes and see Your heart's reflection;
Ever since I was a child I have lived Your resurrection.

Peer into my mind and find our desires are the same;
We seek eternal life for all, we pray for an end to pain.

Reach Your fingers down and gently touch my life;
Catch me if I stumble when surrounded by human strife.

Take my hand and lead me onward, nearer to Your throne;
Peel away the layers of my precious comfort zone.

Lend a shoulder to be cried on when all is going wrong;
Embrace my battle-weary soul and fill it with new song.

Hold high the light of hope, when hope is seemingly lost;
Reveal again the love You showed when hanging from the cross.

Mark the path of Your footsteps that they might show me the way;
Nudge me with Your shepherd's rod if I begin to stray.

Bestow my heart with wisdom when I take to my knees in prayer;
Lead me on to the road less traveled and guide me while I'm there.

Teach me how to follow blindly, never attempting to understand;
For Your wisdom is beyond comprehension, and Your presence is my right hand.

Open my eyes to the miracles, to the promises that have now come true;
And over the years as my heart matures, bring me closer and closer to You.

Sandy, the sixteen-year-old daughter of Cindy and Bill MacNabb, is the granddaughter of Jim and Mary O'Callaghan.

Joy to You!! — 1994, Mary and Jim

Christmas is not the beginning! Elohim, absolute deity, revealed His Name as "I AM," "Yahweh," the ever-existing and everlasting God! The first three verses of Genesis introduce Creator God and His brooding Spirit and His creative Word, unified in the Hebrew plural form Elohim. This spirit realm preceded the beginning of time. Israel regularly affirms the One true God in what is called the Shema, and states, "Hear, O Israel: The LORD our God, the LORD is One." (Deuteronomy 6:4, NIV). This Hebrew word for "one," indicating composite, not only proclaims monotheism but allows for diversity in unity, which is consistent with the Christian revelation of One God in three persons, Father, Son and Holy Spirit.

The Apostle John begins his Gospel account (literally), "In the beginning was the Word, and the Word was with (or towards) the God, and the Word was God." Being with the God, He was also the same essence as God. It is difficult for us who have not experienced the exquisite joys of Heaven to comprehend the amazing sacrifice of God the Father in sending His only begotten Son into a corrupted creation to reconcile it once again into the likeness of Heaven. It is difficult for us to comprehend the amazing sacrifice of God the Son in emptying Himself of heavenly glory to become flesh and dwell among sinful and disobedient mankind. It is difficult for us to comprehend the amazing sacrifice of God the Holy Spirit in consenting to be poured forth from the presence of the Father to dwell in the hearts of men. When generation suffered degeneration, God's united heart called for regeneration! Thus we have Christmas, the precursor to a new creation! The Word became flesh and was tempted like as we are. As the Lamb of God He was sacrificed according to plan, resurrected from the dead, and raised to found a new creation in which all mankind could participate at will. This new birth into the New Kingdom offers empowerment by the indwelling Holy Spirit, so that we can rejoice with exceeding great joy in the fullness of the godhead!

In the fullness of time, Christmas occurred. In the fullness of time the trumpet will blow, calling the Bride of Christ to the marriage feast. In the fullness of time, Jesus will return to set up His earthly, millennial kingdom. After the great white throne judgment the family of God will forever dwell together in exultant love, the adopted children as joint heirs with the begotten Son! Inexpressible joy is the essence of Christmas! Taste of the fullness!

The Government Shall Be Upon Whose Shoulder?

Though Jim lost his right leg below the knee in January and has continued in almost constant pain, we know that love and prayers have sustained us. He is able to walk briefly around the house with two prostheses, and I am happy staying at home with him. His loving daughters have come to Papa-sit, allowing me to make my sixth pilgrimage to Israel and to attend my annual End-Time Handmaidens and Servants World Convention, this time in Dallas, as well as the PCIM (Pat Carver) annual conference at Epworth-by-the-Sea at St. Simons. Our PCIM tour to Israel was my first in the spring, and we even found some places I had never been before. It is a small country, but mighty in the destiny of the world, for God's heart is there and His eyes are ever upon her. The Bible commands us to *"Pray for the peace of Jerusalem"* (Psalm 122:6)!

We give thanks for our family of thirty-one who came for Thanksgiving (all but Amy and hers), and for all our wonderful friends. Happy 1995!

Modlins' Christmas 1995

Myriad changes characterized the year. A few major ones surrounded by the typical minor ones are measured best in reflective hindsight.

Eightieth birthday celebration for Papa ("Dad O'C"). What excitement as relatives and friends from near and far shared in the event — in person, by mail, or via videotape.

Reunion (my twentieth high school reunion, in Naples). How good to see some of those who were key in my life during that time. And what an unexpected blessing to be the guests lavishly hosted by friend Tee and her husband Alphonso while there.

Ropes course. Thad's fourth-grade class visited a ropes course where they learned to work as a team on the "low" elements and then challenged themselves to the max on the "high" elements. I've never been prouder!

Y'all come! We're a "happening place." Come happen with us. We'll fill your home with "furniture from Hickory" and your bellies with food (of some variety).

Children are a blessing from the Lord. So says the Proverb, and we joyfully concur (at least *most* of the time). They are growing so fast, it's a challenge not to rely on yesterday's news for who they are today.

Healthy, ... and wise. (Gee, I think there is something missing in the middle. Oh well, it must not be important.) We are all thankfully healthy. Gene's dad has had a tough year healthwise with two surgeries, but he's bounced back and they're back to their old "no-moss-growing-under-our-feet" schedule. We left my dad feeling pretty good two weeks ago, and Mom in her joyful good health.

R-r-r-r-um. Life is full of unexpected pauses, just like this letter. (Remember this is the third "r"!)

Important events. Gene is finally in his new office, and it has really been a blessing. Hayes was chosen for a special "summer school," which was quite an honor and which he loved. Thad won the Den Pinewood Derby, finished second at Districts, and made it through several rounds at the Council level.

The Government Shall Be Upon Whose Shoulder?

Sports continue to involve us in many ways. Ski report: Big February trip to Colorado for Gene and me with friends. Gene, formerly a novice, is progressing nicely; Laurie, formerly intermediate, regressing dreadfully (but we haven't given up all hope yet). Thad is joining the skiing throngs and has already gone once this fall. Both boys played baseball and soccer. Hillary began her extra-curricular life this fall with "dance" class. After ten weeks, she's ready to move on to gymnastics. I still hit the tennis courts on occasion, and we both stick in with church volleyball. What is it that makes me almost forget to mention fly-fishing? It remains entrenched as Gene's "extracurricular," and judging by the amount of equipment, I guess it's here to stay!

Thanksgiving is always a thanks-filled time as the O'Callaghans gather in Jacksonville and the Modlins in Lincolnton. Our little family spends Thanksgiving with my family (this year there were twenty-two of us) and looks forward to Christmas morning with Gene's.

Missionaries are playing a growing role in our family. Our good friends, the Riches, who serve in Kenya, spent a couple days with us, and then we've had several other missionaries in for meals over the year. It's been a privilege to meet these new friends and add them to those we pray for through the years.

Atlanta wedding: Niece Becky (Cindy and Bill MacNabb's eldest) married Roy Eyre this August. It's not just coincidence that they follow "M" for Missionaries — that's what they hope will be in their future.

Saviour! "For unto you is born this day ... a Saviour, which is Christ the Lord" (Luke 2:11). Rejoicing this season and always in the birth of Jesus.

Our love is sent to you with this Christmas greeting.
Laurie, Gene, Thad, Hayes and Hillary

Merry Christmas — 1995; from Jim and Mary O'Callaghan

"Oh, taste and see that the LORD is good; blessed is the man who trusts in Him!" (Psalm 34:8, NKJV). Jesus said, "I AM the Bread of Life. He who comes to Me shall never hunger" (John 6:35, NKJV). Traditional Hebrew blessings to God start, "Baruch atah, Adonai Eloheinu, Melech HaOlam..." "Blessed art Thou, O Lord our God, King of the Universe..." and then follows the particular praise blessing for the occasion. At a meal, the blessing continues, "ha motzi lehem min ha aretz" ("who brings forth Bread from the earth"). Jesus said, "Unless a grain of wheat falls into the ground and dies, it remains alone; but if it dies it produces much grain" (John 12:24, NKJV). "He who feeds on Me will live because of Me. This is the Bread which came down from Heaven..." (John 6:57-58, NKJV). God planted the seed of His divine Son in an earthen vessel that a Child might be born, a Son given (Isaiah 9:6). Taking the sin of the world upon Himself, the Son tasted death for everyone and was buried and brought forth from the earth, the eternal Saviour! The Gospel of the King of Glory, who reigns eternally over the universe, is thus hidden in the mealtime blessing repeated, knowingly or unknowingly, in Jewish homes regularly!

The angel Gabriel instructed Mary to name her Son Yeshua, "Saviour." "He will be great, and will be called the Son of the Highest; and the Lord God will give Him the throne of His father David. And He will reign over the house of Jacob [Israel] forever, and of His kingdom there will be no end" (Luke 1:31-33). In a dream an angel told Joseph to call His name Yeshua (Jesus) "for He will save His people from their sins" (Matthew 1:21, NKJV). The Hebrew word for "salvation" is yeshuah. "And they shall call his name Emmanuel, which being interpreted is, God with us" (Matthew 1:23, quoted from Isaiah 7:14).

It is no accident that the city of David was called Beth-lehem, "House of Bread," where the child Jesus was born, God's divine Son given. Jesus said that the bread He gives is His flesh and that he who eats His flesh and drinks His blood has eternal life! (John 6:54). At His last Passover celebration with His disciples, Jesus took the bread, broke it and said, "Take, eat; this is My body... do this in remembrance of Me." He also took the cup after supper, saying, "This is the new covenant in My blood. This do, as often as you drink it, in remembrance of Me" (1 Corinthians 11:24-25, NKJV).

The Government Shall Be Upon Whose Shoulder?

On my seventh pilgrimage to Israel (November 8-17), it was "NO little town of Bethlehem for us."

Tourism is the primary industry in Israel. The first Christmas after world pressure forced Bethlehem to be surrendered to the Palestinian Authority, Arafat welcomed Christian pilgrims with a two-story portrait of himself hanging in Manger Square facing the Church of the Nativity. He has declared Jesus to be a Palestinian Arab! My Bible calls it Bethlehem of Judea, City of David, not of the West Bank! The opposing pressures are forcing many Christian Arabs to leave the Bethlehem businesses and homes they have known for generations. Though our government hands out many of our tax dollars to help create and bolster this ungodly terrorist regime, in the land of our only friend and the only democracy in the Middle East, we did not choose to go where Jews and Christians are targeted as "infidels" to be destroyed!

There were forty of us, including a Messianic rabbi and some of his congregation, as well as two Baptist pastors. Thirty of them had never been to the Holy Land before. It was a time for us Christians to get back to our Jewish roots in our Jewish Messiah. It was also a time of national mourning for Prime Minister Rabin. His grave on Mt. Hertzl, where Jewish dignitaries are buried, was covered with flowers and surrounded by many lighted candles and mourners young and old. Zeal in Jewish hearts for the land the God of Abraham, Isaac and Jacob promised to Israel clashes with the strong desire for peace. The Islamic world, sworn to Israel's annihilation, not only encircles her but threatens from within. God's end-time prophetic clock started ticking when Israel became a nation on May 14, 1948. Peace will come only when the Prince of Peace returns!

Jim and I celebrated our eightieth and seventy-fifth birthdays this summer and have tasted and seen that the Lord is good! We hope you have too. It is what makes Christmas merry and gives life for Happy New Years!

Hallelujah!
Be blessed!

Christmas 1995 — from the Regases

"Then He who sat on the throne said, 'Behold, I make all things new.' And He said to me, 'Write, for these words are true and faithful' " (Revelation 21:5, NKJV).

Dear Family and Friends,

Merry Christmas (slightly past) and a Happy New Year! May Christ be enthroned anew in your hearts and lives. It is always such an adventure and a joy to have something new ... new possession, new opportunity, new reckoning of time. I am amazed at the constant grace of these little renewals in our lives, and of how they remind us of the ultimate joy of complete re-creation in Christ. How often we could despair at our constant failings and inadequacy, except for the hope of new beginnings! The God who poured Himself into finite time and space in the person of Jesus has come to create a new creature of us ... one no longer separated from the presence of God by sin and death. "Therefore, if any one is in Christ, he is a new creation; old things have passed away; behold, all things have become new" (2 Corinthians 5:17, NKJV).

Well, as many of you know already, for the Regas family 1995 has been a banner year of celebrating the "new!"— new house, new job, new church, new decade. (Yikes — "forty" found me on December 13!) As with most change, there is the pain of uncertainty ... fortunately counterbalanced by the exhilaration of adventure! Let me catch you up with a quick overview.

Home. While planning and saving to build on our lot, in October we found a house one street over with more space than we could imagine! Although needing a host of "touch-ups," it is wonderful compared to the host of decisions and time required for building new. We started moving in the day after Christmas, and every day that we chip away at unpacking boxes it feels more like home. As further confirmation that this was the right decision for us, the week after we went under contract for this one, someone called out of the blue and bought our lot! ... Nice to keep in mind as we wait for a buyer for our old house.

Job. Still developing: Chris has three projects for residential developments in progress and enjoys working with his dad and two partners on this. Only now, it takes on after-hours status to his new position as director of marketing for

The Government Shall Be Upon Whose Shoulder?

Bastech Chemical Company. The opportunity arose to work for longtime family friends Kitty and Ray Basso in their business, which services the paper manufacturing industry. I have admired Chris as he has jumped into this entirely new arena, no regrets, no looking back, and full speed ahead with a vision for sales and the future at Bastech. A BIG adjustment after working for himself for eight years ... but then again, how hard is it to get used to a regular paycheck again?!

Church. We're very excited to be part of an Orthodox mission church that is very evangelically minded (St. Justin's, a part of the Orthodox Church of America, which has Russian Orthodox "roots," but less ethnic "leaves" and "branches"!). It was difficult to leave dear friends at St. John's, but we still feel connected and much at peace with planting in this new vineyard. Our church hosted a thought-provoking seminar with Frank Schaeffer in September where many Christians in Jacksonville learned more about their Christian heritage from the first thousand years of Church history. I even made an appearance on the local PTL show LIVE broadcast (with Father Ted, Chris and our church "Reader," Andrew) to plug the event... For those who know me well, a definite move of God, eh? It is exciting to be reading, learning and living this Orthodox life in Christ!

Family. Aaaah! Nothing so new on this front; but an exciting milestone as we celebrated our twentieth anniversary in June!

Anastasia. Seventeen, a junior, starting to think about colleges (interests in v-ball scholarship/stock brokerage/architecture/interior design); Bolles volleyball made it to State finals; now playing on an elite traveling team that may go to tourneys in Texas, Colorado, and around Florida; active in Christian youth groups and missions; throws an awesome disco party — three hundred of her "closest" friends, from seven high schools, at our empty old house!

Meredith. Fifteen, a freshman, loving high school social life; moved up to varsity volleyball early in season and even got to contribute to the state championship effort; looking forward to dating on the horizon; made the elite team for traveling v-ball.

Lloyd. Twelve, seventh grade at middle school, big year, as it's his first time for team sports! — football, now basketball, next baseball; Dad still coaches his recreational league sports, so it's a year of double sports (and Chris learning how to watch from the sidelines).

Allison. Seven, second grade, is in Brownies; basketball, may try soccer; loves animals and friends, and helping Mom and Dad (and anyone else); still patiently sharing a room with Zoie.

Mary M. O'Callaghan

Zoie. Three, claims to be four; preschool two days (we both love it!); a whirlwind with a big smile and a lot of acting ability, with her own direction in life!

As for me, my work is cut out for me, unpacking seventeen years' worth of boxes and helping this big 1960s house turn the corner toward the year 2000! — all of this, without mentioning the usual car pools, laundry, sports and meals. I'm still privileged to be the one who has Mom and Dad close by, and so much enjoy my visits with Dad over lunch with "Perry Mason." We get together with Chris's parents at kids' games, frequent dinners together, and now JAGUARS games! Life is good!

We loved hearing from all of you and hope to see more of you this year — hey, there's even room for you to visit, and did I mention that we have a pool now? See you soon!

Best quote of Christmas: Allison (while wearing the King Herod crown that Lloyd wore in the church pageant, and looking at herself in the mirror): "I'm the King of the Jews!"

Zoie (standing next to her, not to be outdone): "And I'm the king of the MILK!"

Joyous Christmas — 1996, from Jim and Mary O'Callaghan

"*Unto us a Child is born, unto us a Son is given*" (Isaiah 9:6, NKJV). The prophet Isaiah looked ahead many years through the corridors of time to proclaim the birth of God's Son on Earth. IT IS A FAMILY MATTER! Celebrate! Jim and I look back through the corridors of time to this, our fifty-fifth celebration together of that unspeakably awesome divine event! Because of His birth our family can celebrate as a well-beloved branch of God's own family. Incredible!

My Randolph-Macon roommate asked for an update on our family, so I'll try to be brief in unraveling any confusion. Marky and Ron Underwood have three children each. The youngest is Benjie MacNabb, co-oping his education at Auburn. Marky's middle daughter is Amy Hughes; she and Billy Joe have two little girls, Kristen and Taylor. Marky's oldest is Lisa McGregor, married to Bill and living in Lutherville, Maryland while working on her M.D. and Ph.D. degrees from Johns Hopkins. Ron's three are all young adults, Sheri, Ronnie and Michael. Ron will retire from Delta Airlines in April, and they are building a house at Amelia Island, an hour from us.

Jimbo and Leah live in Jonesboro, Georgia, and he practices medicine at Fort McPherson. Sarah is now a high school graduate. Leah has been fighting her battle with cancer, which we pray is successfully conquered.

Karen Barnes has cut the marriage ties. She took Danielle and Ryon to Mexico while she studied Spanish for six weeks on the University of Alabama program where she is working on her master's. She hopes to get a job teaching in Jacksonville when she finishes this summer. Danielle has a merit scholarship to Florida State University, and Ryon is still in high school.

Cindy's husband, Bill MacNabb, is President of Dealers Supply Company, the company Jim started in Atlanta. Their oldest daughter, Becky, who is married to Roy Eyre, graduated from Georgia Tech (as did Lisa and her husband Bill), and now teaches. Jim is thrilled with his Tech rooters. Sandy is a sophomore at Appalachian University, and visits with Laurie in nearby Hickory. Emily is in high school.

Wendy and Chris Regas live in Jacksonville for us to enjoy regularly. Anastasia has just been awarded a full volleyball scholarship to Syracuse.

Mary M. O'Callaghan

Meredith is also varsity volleyball at Bolles as a sophomore. With Lloyd's seasonal sports, and even eight-year-old Allison's, they bounce from game to game and even city to city! Zoie, our youngest grandchild, turned four and keeps everybody hopping. Chris has just started a new career as President and CEO of Forke Credit Corporation.

Laurie and Gene Modlin entertain all the families who travel to Hickory for their furniture needs (and some for dental work at the right price!). Dr. Gene is super! Thad, Hayes and five-year-old Hillary are all in the same school this year. They manage to get to Jacksonville two or three times a year.

Jim is under Hospice care, which is great. The pain is too great to use his prostheses, except to transfer, so he mostly lives in his lift chair. Too rarely can I get him into his mobile Rascal to ride around the block. One or more of the girls stays with him when I go to the End-Time Handmaidens Convention (this year in Chicago), or somewhere else (like Israel). I don't "get" to church, but we are church, and praise the Lord for all His goodness to us. Orange Cat, our visiting resident who adopted us, rounds out the family. I met the neighbor who had inherited him from a sick friend, and he bequeathed him to us.

We are preparing for the soon to come Wedding Feast, when the Heavenly Bridegroom comes for His Bride! The trumpet will blow and we will rise to meet Him in the air (1 Thessalonians 4:16,17). You see, IT'S A FAMILY MATTER! Celebrate!

The Modlin Herald News — 1996 Edition

(Published annually. Circulation seventy.)

January. We were merrily enjoying the beginning of the New Year when ... BAM... the ice storm of '96 hit. For hours we sat huddled 'round the gas fireplace, powerless (literally and figuratively) as we listened to the relentless shotgun C-R-A-C-K of limb after ice-laden limb plummeting to its splintery death. For fun we played "Three Little Pigs" as we went to stay with one set of friends then all scurried to yet another friend's house when it also lost power, as had the first. When all was said and done, twenty-four of us were sleeping under the last unfortunate friend's roof! That was the fun part; the-not-so fun part was our tree-crushed van, our limb-speared roof, our broken furnace and our about-to-explode hot water heater. Happy New Year!?!

February. With our temporarily patched van, we headed north to Snowshoe, West Virginia, for a ski weekend with Thad and friends. As you may remember, it was still undecided as to whether or not I liked skiing. But we had a very nice time, so Gene's dream of this being our family sport is still, at least for the time being, alive.

March. Our precious princess (and fearless commandant) Hillary turned five. She told me later that she knew she was five but she felt like she was nine. That sums up our daughter.

April. Easter in Atlanta, then a nice visit with Mom and Dad in Jacksonville. Hayes and Thad won their Cub Scout Pack Pinewood Derby.

May. Hayes turned eight and remains a basically happy, nice guy. Loves soccer, likes baseball, is adding tennis and continues with piano. (Art lessons were added in the fall.)

June. School's out and it is a happening month! Gene and I went whitewater rafting on the New River; much fun (and cold) but a little tamer than expected. June 11, Gene turned forty! (He needed his age to match his distinguished-looking hoary head!) Coincidentally we decided, in about forty-eight hours, to put our house immediately on the market and buy a house. We ended up changing our minds, but not before we took a full ride on that emotional roller coaster. We're sticking with hopes to build a Gene-designed house a few blocks away. The same week,

Mary M. O'Callaghan

Hayes broke his arm, Thad left for a week-long nature/outdoor camp, and sister Karen and I headed for Jacksonville to be with Dad while Mom attended a convention.

July. We had our family vacation in Jacksonville. A great time was had by all, especially with Dad feeling miraculously better.

August. Gene's folks celebrated their fiftieth wedding anniversary with a weekend family gathering in Raleigh. What a special event to share in! School starts, and for the first time in years "Mom" is at home alone. Not to worry, I'm adjusting nicely. Thad begins his last year in elementary school. He's still an introspective, nonaggressive sort with built-in caution, which keeps him out of trouble for the most part. I enjoy greatly time alone with him (translation: sometimes with the WHOLE family he can stir things up!) He does well in school and is becoming a good creative writer. He does the same extracurriculars as Hayes.

September. You'll never believe it, but we were invited by an oral surgeon to go on a seven-day Alaskan cruise. With the GRACIOUS help of family and friends to keep kids, off we went. I cannot begin to express how incredibly blessed we still feel to have experienced all that we did. From the northern lights to the whales; from walking on glaciers to fishing with bears; from the quaint cities to the fun of cruise ship life — it was all an incomparable joy!!!

October. Another big trip, but this one was on the books for a year. Us, the kids, Disney World, five days — great memories were made.

November. Another fun "O'C" wedding in Atlanta as my closest cousin married a dentist. (What good taste!) Then on to Jacksonville where thirty of us celebrated Thanksgiving together, highlighted by a Christmas sing-along in Papa's room. (If you've stuck with us this long, you either really love us or your social life needs to be examined for its entertainment value.)

December. Can anything overshadow the wonder of God's joy and love in giving His only Son to come to Earth so there can be a reason to say "Peace on earth" and "Joy to the world, the Lord is come; let earth receive her King?" The answer is ... NO!!! May you have a joyful, peace-filled Christmas and a God-blessed New Year.

With much love,
Laurie, Gene, Thad, Hayes and Hillary

Merry Christmas 1996; from the Regas Family!

We are filled with the wonder of God's grace all around us... His love poured out in the very air we breathe, food which sustains us, a spouse that encourages, aggravations that stretch us, and children that bless us. We are hungry, and He feeds us. We are hungry for spiritual food, and He pours Himself out, the Bread from Heaven. What can be our response but *"O come, let us adore Him, Christ the Lord"*?

Ours has been a year with some unexpected blessings, so let me catch you up on our news:

Chris. Had an interesting year learning the chemical business with Bastech and good friends Kitty and Ray Basso. It is challenging to move into an entirely new industry, but Chris was pleased with the opportunity there. Then in September, an unexpected, unsolicited offer came from the local Caterpillar dealer: to return to his first love, the world of finance, as founder, President and CEO of a national commercial finance company. Forke Credit Corporation was born in October as a subsidiary of Forke Brothers Auction Company, owned by the CAT dealers here and in Nashville. It has been a whirlwind ever since ... putting away those khakis and dusting off the suits and ties! The creative energy and exhilaration is a real joy, as we renewed contacts with old business friends. *"Eye hath not seen, nor ear heard, neither have entered into the heart of man, the things which God hath prepared for them that love Him"* (1 Corinthians 2:9).

Wendy. I've had some interesting additions to my life, too... a twenty-quart stockpot, and an extra set of flatware to make it through the day! Oh, and four pairs of reading glasses so that as my arm continues to shrink too short to see, and my addled brain forgets where I put the glasses, I am only a drawer away from a better perspective on life. What more do I need?

Anastasia. If it was a juicy Cheeseburger of a year for Chris, it was a Whopper for our eighteen-year-old senior. (No way do we have a child that old?!?) A big fall of recruiting calls, letters and trips, with scholarship offers from Syracuse, Furman, UNF, Rollins and several smaller schools. She and I enjoyed a trip to Syracuse in November to weigh the cold weather and distance versus the $100,000, four-year full ride (tuition, books, room and

Mary M. O'Callaghan

board) and the chance to play a challenging Big East Conference schedule. Guess what? — a down jacket works, and what's a four-hour plane trip?! Go, BIG ORANGE! Anastasia was also just named Player of the Year for north Florida, with a nice article in the paper. If she is going to make us feel old, it's nice that she makes us quite proud!

Meredith. Sweet fifteen … and counting the weeks, days, hours 'til January 3, when she can wrestle Anastasia for the keys to the ol' Volvo. (Good luck!) Meredith has had a strong year academically, juggling honors courses and demanding volleyball schedules. An unexpected pleasure came, as she was the only sophomore player to receive Honorable Mention in the newspaper! Her artistic and literary talents continue to blossom and we see her making conscientious efforts to cultivate Christian virtues, for which we are most proud.

Lloyd. Officially joined the "teenage" ranks last April, but has managed to retain a cheerful demeanor so far! Still losing baby teeth; heading for braces; going to cotillion dances; waging war in "Capture the Flag" with friends; playing foot-, basket- and base-ball (if it has the word "ball" in it, it is all-American and Dad-approved. Anything else is a "foreign sport" to Chris, and akin to Communist infiltration). Dad still coaches or assists recreationally, and Lloyd still lets him! As far as school goes, we see lots of "A's." (Why should he show us the other stuff?) Life is sweet at the top of the middle school heap.

Allison. At eight and one-half, still the Queen of Hospitality and Helpfulness, but makes no bones about counting how many years it will be 'til the ranks thin out and she can have her own room! Loves third grade, animals, art, basketball, volleyball and her family.

Zoie. Sometimes I think her name should have had a "J" instead of a "Z," but she is definitely full of both. There is never a doubt about what she thinks — it's all over her face, and filled with expressive enthusiasm. When she turned four on November 12, she announced, "I changed my mind, I'm twelve." Sometimes she complains that she hasn't done something "for ears and ears." Her teacher has an odd look as she tells me that Zoie is quite entertaining. As she romped with the boys on the playground fort, she waved the girls off, hollering "Go away, we don't like girls!" And this is the child I am counting on to be my ballerina!?!

Other highlights of the year included family wedding celebrations in St. Louis (complete with World Series Cardinal games) and Atlanta, which brought back warm memories in our old downtown Presbyterian Church, where I was raised.

The Government Shall Be Upon Whose Shoulder?

Most of our immediate family gathered for Thanksgiving at Mom and Dad's, complete with Christmas carols around Papa's bedroom chair. "Therefore we do not lose heart, but though our outer man is decaying, yet our inner man is being renewed day by day" (2 Corinthians 4:16, NASB). We marvel at Papa's humor and spirit (as we do at mother's patient caregiving), and are thankful for each day we are privileged to share the umbrella of Dad's love.

I'll close with a quote from a book which has meant a lot to me: "All that exists is God's gift to man, and it all exists to make God known to man, to make man's life communion with God. It is divine love made food, made life, for man" (*For the Life of the World*, by Alexander Schmemann).

Rejoicing with you in *"the Bread of God ... who comes down from Heaven and gives life to the world"* (John 6:33, NIV).

Chris and Wendy

Unpublished Letter to *The Florida Times-Union*

August 7, 1997

Letters from Readers

Americans, who have been Constitutionally guaranteed the right to freedom of speech, are volubly expressing opposite interpretations of that Constitution as to the "separation of church and state." The extreme demands of the left-wing interpretation go so far as to deny the right of free speech to those who express a godly view, while at the same time declaring it a matter of "free speech" for radicals to despise America by publicly burning our flag for which our patriots have bled and died!

HAS AMERICA GONE MAD?

On every piece of American money, America declares, "IN GOD WE TRUST." To our detriment and shame America has denied this very GOD in whom we trust! Let there be no mistaking who this GOD is, in whom our very government has so publicly declared our trust: He is the GOD of Abraham, Isaac and Jacob, the eternal Creator GOD revealed in the Holy Bible. He is the FATHER GOD who gave His SON to redeem all mankind, the Messiah Yeshua, Jesus. He is not Allah. He is not Buddha. He is none of the myriads of Hindu gods. He is not the goddess Gaia, Mother Earth, or any other of the mythological and New Age characters. He is not Satan, the prince of the adversaries. Most importantly, he is not mere MAN, whom humanists seek to place on a divine pedestal for worship. He is the Creator God, now ruling the universe, whom our American forefathers trusted to rule this nation in perfect accord with His written WORD, the HOLY BIBLE. Can we, a nation blessed by GOD, or should we trust this ONE that every coin or piece of scrip declares is trustworthy?

The first main breach in this declared trust occurred when our American government denied our schoolchildren the right to read the Bible, or mention the Name, or thank this God for the blessings of the day. Atheism, with the help of irresolute Christian and Jewish leaders, gained a place of legality in our nation. From that first denial of trust by our Supreme Court, we have seen the decline of our once great nation. "Secular humanism," declared by our Supreme Court to be

The Government Shall Be Upon Whose Shoulder?

a religion, is now the religion openly and unashamedly taught and celebrated in our schools and public institutions. Our nation's Founding Fathers have joined the ranks of the vilified "right-wing extremist Christians." From our courtrooms, where witnesses were required to place their right hand upon the HOLY BIBLE and swear to tell the truth, the whole truth and nothing but the truth "so help me GOD," judges have ordered the removal of the TEN COMMANDMENTS from the walls. There is a great lack of the spirit of the Fear of the LORD in our land! Is it too late for America?

I say "NO!" The only strategy that can bring this nation from the brink of destruction by anti-God forces is to quit trusting in our money, but to trust in the GOD whom we proclaim on that money! Shall we please GOD or shall we cater to the votes of Satanists, atheists, sodomites, lesbians, child-sacrificing hedonists, thieves (in and out of government!) and everyone who dissents from the GOD of the BIBLE? Those who fail to govern by our Constitution, as based on biblical precepts, but govern by ungodly activists' opinions should be impeached, including ungodly judges. Our Constitution has made provision for such impeachment. Without God we are creating hell on Earth! The GOD "IN WHOM WE TRUST" is TRUSTWORTHY!

"O Jerusalem, Jerusalem..."
(Matthew 23:37)
Mary O'Callaghan, November 1997

Why would any thinking person, year after year, make the arduous journey into a land like Israel, where seeds of hatred have been purposefully nurtured by proclamations of genocide from multitudinous surrounding foes, a purpose insidiously carried out by acts of terrorism? To answer this question one must address the question "What is life all about and how does one find fulfillment?"

The Jew seeks the answer in the Hebrew Scriptures, the *Tanakh*, which we call The Old Testament or Covenant. These are the same Scriptures that Jesus quoted *"It is written..."* and obediently followed. The Jews at the time of Jesus were well-schooled in their Scriptures and their oral traditions; consequently they were aware of the prophecy of Jeremiah 31:31 that the LORD was going to *"make a new covenant with the house of Israel, and with the house of Judah."* Jesus demonstrated to them that that time had come as He shared His Passover meal with His disciples in an upper room (Luke 22:14 ff). And after He was crucified, dead and buried, and rose again, He explained to two followers on the road to Emmaus all the things in those Hebrew Scriptures concerning Himself, beginning with Moses and all the prophets (Luke 24:25-27). The Church has adopted this New Covenant as their own, and rightly so, since we are grafted into the Hebrew roots; but it was promised to and instituted for Israel! Years of persecution of Jews by the misguided church have separated them from this New Covenant, making it an offense to them. Jeremiah 31:34 explains that they shall no longer teach each other, *"saying, Know the LORD, for they shall all know Me ... saith the LORD: for I will forgive their iniquity, and I will remember their sin no more."* The LORD declares that when He puts His teaching in their innermost being and upon their hearts, then He will be their God and they will be His people! Messianic congregations are springing up, attesting to that glorious truth, while Christian congregations are repenting of past injustices and finding their Jewish roots!

Many Christians, as well as believing Jews, are dedicated to making the LORD "known" by His natural chosen people, whom the Bible de-

The Government Shall Be Upon Whose Shoulder?

scribes as stiff-necked! No way has the Church replaced God's natural family, but has been adopted into it; and from the Church, Father God is seeking a Bride for His Son! When every tongue and nation has heard the Good News of the New Covenant, ratified by the blood of Jesus that was shed for ALL who will receive Him, then Jesus will come for His Bride, who is even now preparing herself for the wedding festivities! Repentant love is the ingredient for that preparation!

In following the mandate to make Jesus known, I have just returned from my ninth pilgrimage of almost a month in Israel with two friends. We went to pray, comfort the saints, bless Israel, love the people, celebrate the Feast of Tabernacles with the International Christian Embassy, Jerusalem, and follow the Lord's leading.

My precious Jim was blessed on January 22 to join His Lord in Heaven (Revelation 14:13). He is **greatly** missed!!! Karen, Ryon and Danielle have moved in with me. The whole family will celebrate Thanksgiving together at Wendy's. I take this early opportunity to wish you MERRY CHRISTMAS and pray that you, too, KNOW the Lamb of God, our Jewish Messiah, in a precious personal way!

Merry Christmas;
from Cindy and Bill MacNabb — 1998

Dear family and friends,

After a few hours spent during this "low-key" time of the year, trying to master this new publishing program that failed to include directions for dummies, I can swap my "Bah humbug for technology" for "Hallelujah! It's Christmastime!"

Ninety-eight has been an exciting year for the MacNabbs. Becky and Roy (Eyre) have made the transition to Calgary, Canada, with seeming ease. They are pleased with their jobs with Wycliffe Bible Translators, with their new house, and with the prospect of becoming new parents in June. If you have not received their newsletter, we'll be glad to send you a copy.

Sandy is at that exciting and terrifying point of trying to figure out how to translate dreams and visions into reality. She has found a wonderful facility, "Noah's Ark," which is a foster home for up to twelve children, as well as a refuge and rehab facility for animals. She hopes to use the next few months interacting with both children and animals and fine-tuning her goals. She might need to shift to animal husbandry, veterinary school and counseling education... wherever she feels God is leading her. The one thing she is certain of, at this moment, is that this program seems custom-tailored to the desires of her heart.

Emily is also at one of the crossroads in her life. She is at that senior year — ready to transition to ... WHAT? Seriously considering a year in mission work, she might want to develop a program offering inner-city missions experiences to high school students. There's also the possibility of an internship with World Servants. We don't want to overlook any possibilities in Calgary, either. Or she may decide to head on to college. Decisions, decisions!

Bill continues to head up Dealers Supply, which is growing and booming. God has been most gracious. Despite a blip on Bill's health screen, from another seizure — probably from some scar tissue, a reminder of God's healing! — there is no evidence of any active disease process. This does mean we are back on a "no driving" routine, so we are doing our part to support Atlanta carpooling!

What about Cindy? As I type, I have two cockatiels helping with the keyboard and two dogs (one a visitor) trying to get under my chair. Let's not

The Government Shall Be Upon Whose Shoulder?

forget the cat asleep on the bed beside me. I've had a great time getting a "volunteer morning" going at church this fall (keeping bulletin boards, children's classrooms, etc., current, and getting mailings out). I also love working with the kids during children's church. Monday afternoons, I help with a Campfire program for special-needs children. I find getting out to hit a tennis ball occasionally has great therapeutic value. My days are varied and full — just the way I like them.

God is good. We are richly blessed, and we pray that you also are attuned to the many evidences of God's grace in your lives. May blessings abound in '99.

      Love,
      Cindy and Bill, and gang

Christmas Greetings; from the Underwoods!

Regretfully, my personal correspondence habits are not much improved, so here goes the second annual Underwood newsletter.

Ron and I are happily settled into our little "retirement" home here on Amelia Island, and I have almost recovered from resettlement shock. (We all know I adjust slowly to change!) We have some wonderful friends here and are sufficiently bonded so that "homesick for Newnan" attacks are hitting me less frequently. Of course, it helps to have frequent visits from our family and friends. Please know that our standing invitation still stands!

Ron continues to pursue his golfing avocation with single-minded dedication. He is playing in some regional tournaments now — and when he is good enough to tour, maybe I'll be his "groupie." I continue to enjoy my book club, stock club, bridge club and volunteer work. I am a recently trained Guardian Ad Litem and, as such, am doing investigative work and monitoring children who have been removed from unfit homes — rewarding and challenging for me, but it doesn't hold a candle to being a "granny."

My new name is "Mimi," and our latest little bundle of joy is grandson William Joel Hughes, born November 20 to Amy and Billy. Kristen and Taylor are the proud big sisters, and all are doing well. I hear that Kristen, age nine, is a really big help with little brother. The next big event will be mid-January, when daughter Lisa and Bill McGregor are expecting the stork's arrival. They are living in Mebane, North Carolina, a quaint little town located between Greensboro (Bill's Proctor and Gamble) and Durham (where Lisa is a resident at Duke en route to becoming a pediatric oncologist.) Naturally, "Mimi" will head north for that occasion.

Daughter Sheri is selling real estate in Atlanta like hotcakes and is buying her first home — her subdivision's model. We are so proud of her continuing spirituality and maturity; and Dad and Marky are excited to have another place to "lay our heads" in Atlanta. Ronnie and Jennifer have celebrated their first anniversary, added to their house, and stay in a whirlwind of business and civic activities. For the present, their "son" is Tobie J., a black lab — but who knows when that could change? Michael continues working at the golf club here, and it's

The Government Shall Be Upon Whose Shoulder?

really nice having one of ours so close at hand. Son Benjie is graduating from Auburn in March with a major in finance and will start job interviews over the holidays. He aims to stay in the "Deep South!" Praise God, all are healthy and doing well!

Thankfully, both of our Moms are hale and hearty. It's great living close to Mom Mary; and we look forward to a holiday visit from Mom Opal, sister Vicki and her husband Lou — all from Pittsburgh. We'll be going to the Jacksonville-Pittsburgh football game and rooting for our respective teams — go, Jaguars!

We thank God for our many blessings over the past year — most notably for our precious friends and family. May God bless you and yours over this holiday season and throughout the New Year. We send our love!

Marky and Ron

Merry Christmas — 1998, from Mary O'Callaghan

GOD had a plan! It was a marvelous plan because GOD IS LOVE! HE was; HE is; HE will always be! Ever dwelling in eternity, HE planned to execute HIS will in a set period of "time," in a set "space" of HIS creation. The FATHER'S WILL to multiply HIMSELF in earthly sons was expressed by HIS WORD, who agreed to become the sacrificial LAMB as assurance for many sons and daughters in whom the SPIRIT of GOD agreed to dwell. The GODHEAD worked in perfect accord! All contingencies were covered, including rebellion in the heavenlies and rebellion on Earth! FAMILY was the plan and REDEMPTION was the method! REPENTANCE and OBEDIENCE were the means! What a plan!

Just as all the GODHEAD was bound together in the FATHER (the Hebrew word for this composite unity is *echad*), so GOD sees every earthly family as bound together in a father, being "one" (*echad*) with the mother and children! Since FATHER GOD did not want HIS earthly family ignorant of HIS plan, HE INSPIRED many of HIS obedient sons, through the ages, to write HIS plan and instructions for all mankind in HIS Bible. According to the pattern of heavenly unity, GOD, the Master Designer of the universe, instituted a covenant with HIS creation, choosing and committing HIMSELF to Abraham as the father of HIS earthly family. HE renewed HIS covenant with the promised miracle son Isaac, and again with Isaac's son Jacob, whom GOD renamed Israel, "Prince with God." GOD's commitment to HIS family ISRAEL included the promise of a New Covenant with them (Jeremiah 31:31 ff). Why a New Covenant? Because they had broken HIS covenant, though HE was a husband to them! (Isaiah 54:5). GOD remains the pattern for all husbands and fathers!

What is the situation today, as we see GOD's plan approaching a climax? Rebellion in the heavenlies resulted in the covering cherub being banished, taking with him a third of the rebellious angels, to become the Adversary, or Satan. Satan set up his rival kingdom as the "prince of the power of the air," or as JESUS called him, "prince of this world," when the first Adam disobeyed GOD and surrendered to Satan the dominion that GOD had invested in him. In the fullness of time the WORD became flesh in Bethlehem of Judea (not the West

The Government Shall Be Upon Whose Shoulder?

Bank, or Palestine, as the Adversary would have you accept). He grew up in Nazareth, the second Man, or last Adam (1 Corinthians 15:45 f). Following the pattern of the promised miracle son Isaac, JESUS fulfilled the promise of the New Covenant for Israel! HIS total obedience in pouring out HIS blood in temporary surrender to Death, and being resurrected, effected the defeat of Satan, restoring kingdom authority to GOD's family! Satan's power has not yet been stripped from him, though JESUS has regained the authority over all power that Adam lost and transferred it to HIS CHURCH. Satan influences through deception. Some Jewish religious zealots refuse to accept MESSIAH JESUS,;and some zealous Christians maintain that the Jews killed JESUS, so GOD has forsaken them. But He died for all, and in JESUS that middle wall of partition has come down, making one new man (Ephesians 2:14), bringing peace and wholeness to GOD's family, Jew and Gentile! Sadly, the secular and unbelievers remain outside the FAMILY. GOD wants none to perish, but He will not coerce or abrogate one's will. FATHER is calling forth a Bride for JESUS. Let's all prepare for the call.

Another year has passed, and another pilgrimage to the Land of Jesus. Two more great-grandbabies have blessed our family, and two more are on the way! God is good, all the time! May HIS blessings rest on you and yours in 1999!

December 1998 — The Regas family

Dear Family and Friends,

"Warm" Christmas greetings to all, from sunny Jacksonville where summer is enjoying an extended booking! Nineteen ninety-eight has been a kinder, gentler year for the Regas family, for which we are thankful. We hope this season finds you counting your blessings, be they few or many, and looking forward to a new year of growth in faith.

Our year had some bright markers along the road as we became, for the first time for any of us, world travelers. Chris's parents, Frieda and Lloyd, had long wanted to take the extended family on a "roots" trip to Greece. Chris's sister Stephanie became our trip coordinator for a marvelous twelve days of Grecian holiday. While the trip was in the planning stages, we realized that Chris had business in Holland a few days ahead of our departure for Greece ... no way was he going on his first trip to Europe without me; no way was I getting away without a train of five kids... So Stephanie worked some magic and got the seven of us booked to Holland. It was a fairytale. (Some of it was a nightmare, actually, as Chris drove the narrow streets of Amsterdam — going the wrong way on top of the trolley tracks, laughing hysterically and proclaiming out the windows to no one, and everyone, that we were lost on the *straatens* and *grachtens!*) We stayed in the charming port city of Vlissingen, where Forke held an equipment auction. While Chris worked, the kids and I traded our guilders for francs, hopped in the van without a map, and ferried over to Belgium for an enchanted evening in thirteenth-century Bruges. The shoppes were all closing; but we managed to get into one chocolatier, sample the wares, and buy eight pounds of heaven to haul around the airports and hotels of Greece for the next two weeks! ... And it was worth it!

We met his sister Karen, Frieda and Lloyd, and Steph and Peter in Athens, then took a three-day cruise of the islands, each one distinctive — culminating in our tour of the two thousand year old ruins of Ephesus, in Turkey, and back to Athens, the Acropolis, and the start of our "Classical Tour" of the Peloponnisos. Papou Lloyd arranged for a thirty-two-person bus for the twelve of us, and now Zoie thinks our busdriver, Pavlos, is a member of the family! We ran the field at

The Government Shall Be Upon Whose Shoulder?

Olympia, swam the Ionian Sea and collected the glistening pebbles from the beaches, ate bread and lamb and *salata*, crossed the Corinthian Canal... But the highlight of the trip came as we neared Platanos and saw Lloyd's relatives waiting for us at the *taverna* on the seaside street — tears, hugs, plenty of *retsina* from the "Regopoulos" wine vats, and fresh fish for all. ("Para kallo, could you *kopsai ta kefalia* — cut off the heads — for the kids?" The eyebrows up in surprise, "What?! — it's the best for the flavor!") We rode up the mountain to the charming hundred-year-old family home overlooking the blue Gulf, where Chris's grandfather was born, and knew it would forever be a part of us.

To buffer our reentry to reality, back in the United States of America we quickly headed to a family reunion at Amelia Island with Frieda's side of the family — we've never processed so much film in so short a time, but the wonderful memories are etched forever in the silver of our Kodachromes and in our minds. We enjoyed a full-blown reunion this weekend for Lloyd's eightieth birthday when thirty-five of these same fun-loving, family-minded relatives squeezed travel plans into the hectic holidays. We are so blessed!

The O'Callaghans had warm family moments in Atlanta over Thanksgiving, where we could gather around our dear sister-in-law Leah as she fights cancer. Her grace and cheer are an inspiration to all, as is my brother's devoted care.

I've blown my intended one-page letter, but I'll try to be brief with our personal updates.

Anastasia is in her second year at Syracuse, where she broke a Big East Conference record for the most blocks in a single game this season and led the Conference in blocks/game, while continuing on the academic dean's list.

Meredith has had a wonderful senior year, stressed only by the number of committee, yearbook, volunteer and student council activities that she juggles while taking honors and advanced placement courses, all during volleyball season! She was named the Florida High School Coaches' North-east Florida Player of the Year in Division 3A, as well as making Second Team All State, and has had some recruiting options, including an official visit to Big East Villa Nova. Her own team made it to the state Final Four! All that, and Homecoming Court, too! College options remain wide open as she considers walking on at some target schools or attending the University of Florida with some academic scholarship included.

Lloyd just finished his sophomore football season when Varsity won the

Mary M. O'Callaghan

state championship last Thursday! He suffered a growth-plate strain and two-week cast toward the season end, the bright spot being that at six feet two inches, his growth plate is still open and chances of overtaking his Dad's six feet four inches seem very good! He now jumps into basketball. We in the family feel that educators should model learning efficiencies from Lloyd, who despite school and practices 'til 7 PM, is seldom seen having to labor over schoolwork — he claims it's the driver's education study hall time he has!

Allison (ten) begins her fourth season of volleyball, having made the fourteen and under team. (Mom has mixed feelings, but she and Dad are excited.) Her last year of grade school brings Patrols, Hip-Hop Dance class, piano, a dance part in the school *Nutcracker* production, and a straight A record. She already seems like a "tween-ager," but she's still a pretty great kid to have around!

Zoe (a.k.a. "Zoie" — okay, so I'm having second thoughts on how to spell this name) is finally a full-fledged kindergartner as well as a world traveler. As we drove to Tampa for one of Mere's tourneys, she asked, "What language will they speak in this village?" She rounds out her schedule with ballet and a math enrichment class (I'm trying to impart an early love for what I early disdained), aiming for soccer and the world of sports this spring.

Chris is busy with a capital "B," but occasional overlaps of business and hunting are a welcome oasis. Knowing the stress, I appreciate all the more the warm laughter and energy that he brings home to the family. A convention trip to Naples last summer afforded the opportunity to show Allison and Zoe my old hometown as well as take a boat trip on the canals to see the old homestead — even picked limes from "our" tree for a remembrance for Mother (the house was empty and for sale). Chris does love his work and especially the fine people that he works for and with — makes a great environment.

Wendy (to quote radio's Dr. Laura): "I'm my kids' Mom" and couldn't love it more. Still spinning at exercise, still praying, still becoming. And still wishing you the joys of Christ's coming, and the language of His love in your village!

Afterword

This has been the chronicle of one family, looking back over forty years of life and government in America. The family is God's building block for all of society, in all ages, which makes it Satan's most critical objective for destruction. Destroy the family and you have destroyed the nation. Anything, or anyone, that touches the family negatively or destructively is ungodly — the enemy of God.

Those people who are led by the Spirit of God are sons of God (Romans 8:14) and enjoy the family's benefits! They know and rely on God's promises in His Word as eternal truth! Psalm 68 exhorts us to sing to God, extol Him and rejoice before Him! He is a Father of the fatherless and a defender of widows, dwelling in His holy habitation. He sets the solitary in families. As the eternal Father, He delivers His obedient and repentant children from bondage, but allows the rebellious to reap what they have sown.

There is no higher position in the universe than FATHER. Creation begins with FATHER. The first verse in the Bible, Genesis 1:1, introduces us to *Elohim,* Hebrew for "God," which is a plural form of a composite unity, *echad*. The first three verses of Genesis reveal to us the components of this plural unity, called "the Godhead" in the New Covenant, as they united to produce creation together. The will of the Father, was expressed in His spoken Word, empowered by union with His holy breath, or Spirit. (The Hebrew word *ruach,* and the Greek word *pneuma* both mean "spirit," "breath" or "wind.") God said, *"Let US make Adam in Our [own] image, according to [Our] likeness and let **them** have dominion..."* (Genesis 1:26, NKJV). God saw the earthly family as one, *echad,* in the father. The father is head of the family, under the Godhead. The woman, brought forth out of the side of "Adam" to be his "helper" (also a name for the Holy Spirit), in union with the man brings to birth a newly created being after the will of his father! Jews recite daily Deuteronomy 6:4, the *Shema: "Hear, O Israel: The* LORD *our God, the* LORD *is One (echad)."* Only those Jews who have accepted Jesus as Messiah can understand fully this proclamation of the Oneness of the Father, Son and Holy Spirit.

Those modern feminists who demand "sameness" with men do not understand the precious position of women. Just as the Holy Spirit, the promise of God sent to us at the request of Jesus, is our *Paraclete,* the

Mary M. O'Callaghan

"one called alongside" to comfort, convict, empower, teach, strengthen, etc., and be the "Help" we all need, so the woman was called to be the "help," meet or comparable to the man, to walk alongside him, for it was not good for him to be alone (Genesis 2:18).

God, in covenant with Abraham, and renewed with Isaac and with Jacob (Israel), called Himself the "husband" of Israel (Jeremiah 3:14 and 31:32). From this union, by the Holy Spirit, the Word became flesh and dwelt among men, Messiah Jesus! (John 1:1-14). God the Father is now calling forth a Bride for His Son Jesus, for it is not good for Him to be alone! How glorious is the FAMILY structure! It is in understanding this that an earthly father can accept his high position and godly responsibilities in procreation. It is in understanding this that a woman can strive to bring glory to her husband, just as the Holy Spirit glorifies Jesus (John 16:14). It is in the family structure that children can learn obedience and respect and wisdom and knowledge, and yield to a loving father according to the pattern of a loving Father God!

A Tribute

Since this is a book about family, I could not close it without paying tribute to the precious husband God gave me for over fifty-five years. He wasn't perfect, nor am I, nor is there any such thing as a perfect marriage! But he was God-chosen and just right for me! He was very loving, with a keen sense of humor, an essential ingredient in any marriage! He loved his family, even if he didn't feel obligated to go to PTA's, dance or band recitals, camping or such things. He was a "people person," a "man's man," who worked hard and played hard, first at tennis and then at golf, as his doctor directed. He enjoyed his stag bridge, gin rummy and poker games at the club.

Jim loved his native city, Atlanta, to the point of thinking that everyone with any sense should desire to live there. There came a time when big-city life yielded to wonderful village life in our little paradise of Naples, Florida, but Atlanta always had his heart. Seventeen years later, when medical problems prodded us to seek further help, we moved to Jacksonville where Mayo Clinic and our daughter Wendy and family were established. Since his Dad died suddenly at the age of sixty-three with a heart attack, a pillar in the Presbyterian church, Jim always expected to die young, admitting his life was less disciplined and perfect than his Dad's! Besides that, Jim had had a serious heart attack just before he turned forty-five. I refused to give in to such prognostication and he did live to be over eighty-one!

Jim loved his Lord and the Presbyterian church, which he served as a deacon and an elder, and sometimes as a teacher. When he returned from Guam at the close of World War II, I left my Methodist church to join him in his lifetime, downtown Atlanta church, where we brought up our six children. Central Presbyterian was an old, very active church, ministering in the inner city. I was able to work in the sick baby clinic and other daytime activities, as well as sing in the choir and teach Sunday school.

When we moved from Atlanta to Naples we visited different churches, mostly attending an Episcopal church. I was asked to organize a middle school group, so for three years a group of girls met weekly in our home during the school year. Even in Atlanta, I was searching for a church or prayer group moving in the power of God, "doing the same things Jesus did," according to the promises I read in the Bible. I didn't know what you called it, but I finally found what I was hungering for, visiting Charisma Chapel in little Naples! I asked Jesus and was gloriously and joyously baptized in the Holy Spirit! It marked the difference between knowing about God and knowing Him personally. It was somewhat of a threat to Jim, particularly after he invited my little mother to come and live with us and that little Methodist lady fell right into it, raising her hands to praise the Lord with true John Wesley fervor. Daughter Laurie followed suit, wondering why anyone would go to a "regular" church when they could go to Charisma Chapel. Wendy called from Vanderbilt announcing she had received the Holy Spirit, and even our son came back from a year interning in the Navy in Spain saying the doctors and nurses in his prayer group prayed the same way!

When Jim finally joined the Moorings Presbyterian Church, I would attend an early service with him and then head to Charisma Chapel. When he accusingly said I had changed, I said, "I certainly hope so!" He didn't really understand, thinking I had somehow "left the faith," but he gave me freedom to follow my heart and even sent me numerous times to Israel! He was a cordial host to the many wonderful speakers who stayed overnight or for seminars with us while I was president of Women's Aglow. That was a real blessing, in contrast to some husbands who held their wives in the bondage of traditions.

Church was always an important part of our lives, but we never established a family Bible reading or worship time together, nor did we pray together, other than bedtime prayers, table blessings or special occasions. I longed for it but did not want to usurp spiritual leadership. The fifteen-year spread in our children's ages, with numerous schedules and conflicts, didn't encourage family altar, though the children knew our priorities and we tried to lead godly lives before them. We are all strongly knit together and love the Lord. Though he never wanted to go himself, before he died Jim told me how much he appreciated my making Jerusalem very important to him! We can love deeply without hungering for the same things!

Jim also loved his country. He served in the Reserves and retired as a Colonel after twenty years of duty, including five years of active duty during World War II. He didn't believe in asking anyone to do what he wouldn't do, which philosophy also pushed him into political service.

Jim's circulation problems left him increasingly debilitated and in increasing pain. Bypass surgery to the leg helped for a time, but eventually one leg was removed below the knee and he was fitted with a

The Government Shall Be Upon Whose Shoulder?

prosthesis. It was a shock to learn that removing the leg did not remove the pain, for he would feel stabbing pain in a foot that was no longer there! For an ambitious, energetic, competitive, athletic Irishman who had to adjust to a sedentary life of pain and pills, Jim did a marvelous job of uncomplaining adjustment.

We went to Atlanta to see about further pain control, and there the second leg was removed below the knee. It was an entirely new ball game to learn to transfer without either leg. The prostheses were almost too painful to use, and I assured Jim my two legs were sufficient for both of us. Our doctor finally turned him over to Hospice, who could fine-tune his pain control. They graciously served him and helped me for the last sixteen months of his life. I had a blind friend in Naples whom I took on several flights, with her leader dog curled up under the seat in front of us. When she would thank me, I would assure her that she was my opportunity. When Jim lost his legs he said, "I know, you are going to say that I am your opportunity"; and I said, "Well, you are!" And truly it was an opportunity to serve my independent Irishman as never before.

Every morning when I'd go into his room, he'd say, " 'This is the day that the Lord has made; let us rejoice and be glad in it.' Open up the blinds and let the sunshine in." The control this formerly independent man could exercise over his life now consisted of the items within his immediate reach, clickers for his TV and light switches, and a large brass handbell that would resound throughout the house. I had purchased the bell on one of our trips to Clinton, South Carolina, where Jim attended board meetings of Presbyterian College. The wives were taken antique shopping for entertainment. Since I am not really into antiques OR shopping, I participated by buying the least item I could find, which at least could be useful to round up our gang from the neighborhood. It reminded me of Williamsburg. Little did I know that it would rule my life for several years! Sometimes when I answered the summons of the bell, Jim would grin and say, "I just wanted to look at you!" Sometimes the bell would ring and I would say to myself, "Man, I just sat down," but I made a point of never entering his room without a smile. I was almost indignant when asked if I threw that bell away. No, it holds an important place in my room, to remind me of my precious "opportunity"!

I believe the main business of marriage is to uplift and meet the needs of your other half. If you both share that philosophy, you are in reality uplifting yourself, for the two of you are one. This treasure of commitment seems to be lost in a world that spurns godly guidelines.

Jim slept and lived in his electric lift chair. It would have been so easy for him to wallow in self-pity, as he endured constant pain or the aftereffects of pain relief. But he never complained or asked, "God, why me?" His sense of humor bore witness that *"a merry heart doeth good like a medicine"* (Proverbs 17:22). Since it was difficult to manage a daily shave, he had fun growing a beard. It became part of my daily ritual to get a fuzzy kiss and remind him, "Have I told you today how very precious you are to me?" We all need the assurance that we are precious to someone! We **all** are precious to Jesus! Tell it to the lonely!

We had ramps in the house and an electric Rascal, but Jim couldn't get in it by himself, nor sit up very long. He did manage to drive himself around the block several times, with me trotting in hot pursuit calling, "Barney Oldfield, slow down!" He was not morbid, but several times said, "I don't know that the Lord is doing me any favors keeping me here, but He must have a purpose." He could see divine beings in the corner of his room, and as days passed he would confirm to me that they were still there. I was grateful to be with him that early morning when he took off for his new home without me! God is good.

Death is an inescapable part of life unless we are snatched out of here at the sound of the trump! Even when it is expected, in reality it is a shock. We had faced that reality during World War II. We had faced it when Jim had his ruptured appendix, peritonitis and gangrene. We had faced it when our four-engine plane lost two engines on one side. We had faced it with every surgical procedure Jim had to undergo because of his blocked arteries and circulation problems. But Jesus tells us, in John 8:51,52, that if anyone keeps His word he will never see nor taste death. Hebrews 2:14,15 assures us that we can be released from a lifetime of bondage to the fear of death because Jesus has tasted death for us! Wonderful substitute! We won't see or taste death but will step from one life into a more glorious eternal life with Him! What could be more wonderful than that "Blessed Assurance"?

Because I KNOW these things I am sure that I have not been the picture of the typical, grieving widow. Do I miss my beloved husband of many years? You bet! Do I feel sorry for myself? Never! I have tried to live my life to have no regrets, which requires a daily walk of love. Have I failed along the way? You bet! But for the Christian there is the assurance of forgiveness in repentance, blotting out the failures. Jesus

The Government Shall Be Upon Whose Shoulder?

has swallowed up death in victory so we look with excitement for that city made without hands! We are confident that the promises in the Bible are everlasting truth and that our God is a loving Father who waits for us with outstretched arms!

I am eternally thankful for my husband and family and appreciate my years of learning to be a wife, helping me prepare for a heavenly Bridegroom! To you also I say, prepare and look up! Our redemption is drawing nigh!

Year-End Commentary — 1998

The final year of this decade, century and millennium opens on a world of chaos. Weapons of mass destruction have proliferated. Communication technologies have brought the world into close proximity, though widely diverse as to ideologies. Unseen powers manipulate the world economy, pushing towards a New World Order, or one-world government with a single monetary system and a global army to enforce global law. The only thing that stands against this system is the Judeo-Christian faith in the God of Abraham, Isaac and Jacob. God's prophets foretold exactly this situation for the end of days before the Messiah comes, the only One who can bring peace!

Today, in the midst of world chaos, there is no great world leader. When one arises on the scene, promising peace to this stress-ridden, war-torn world, the world will gratefully choose him to reign over them. The Apostle John calls this one the Antichrist, who will take over the world's government for a time. The Apostle Paul calls him the *"man of sin,"* the *"son of perdition"* (2 Thessalonians 2:3). The devil knows his end is sure, and he is exerting all his wiles and power to enlarge his kingdom. The HOME is his prime target. Outer darkness is the place God has prepared for Satan, all his cohorts and every person who stands against God.

Can we know the end? The Bible beckons and pleads with us, as it constantly reiterates *"...that you may know..."* Paul affirms, *"I would not have you ignorant, brethren."* Messianic Jews are placing ads in Israel: "READ YOUR BIBLE!" Should we do less in America? The Bible tells it all! Only godly repentance can bring revival to America. Eternity awaits! Where will you spend it? The choice is yours. There is only one way to the FATHER, and that is through the SON, Jesus Christ. He alone has paid the fine for your sins with His precious blood shed at Calvary. He alone can clothe you with righteousness to stand before the Father without being consumed in holy fire! God's wrath has been pronounced over all evil, and all have sinned and come short of the glory of God. Bow before the King of the universe, turn from every wicked way, and ask Him to circumcise your heart and give you a heart of love toward God and your fellowman. Ask Him to fill you with His precious Holy Spirit that you might be strengthened with all might in the inner man. Then go share the Good News with your family and the lost in the world! They are waiting and they are hungry! Jesus is waiting also!

ℭ Notes ℜ

Under His Wings
6271-24 St. Augustine Rd.
Suite 316
Jacksonville, FL 32217

Notes

Notes

Notes

Notes

Notes

Notes

Notes

Notes

**Copies of this book
may be obtained by writing:**

Under His Wings, Inc.
6271-24 St. Augustine Rd, Ste 316
Jacksonville, FL 32217

Or ask your Christian Book Store.